A SKEPTIC'S GUIDE TO FUNCTIONAL PROGRAMMING WITH JAVASCRIPT

D1343734

James Sinclair

First edition: 25 November 2022
Revised: 28 November 2022
Revised: 3 December 2022
Revised: 11 December 2022

A catalogue record for this
book is available from the
National Library of Australia

ISBN 978-1-4709-7336-0   Paperback
ISBN 978-1-4709-7334-6   Ebook

CONTENTS

vi

ACRONYMS

API	Application Programming Interface
CPU	Central Processing Unit
CSS	Cascading Style Sheets
DOM	Document Object Model
FSM	Finite State Machine
HTML	HyperText Markup Language
JIT	just-in-time
JSON	JavaScript object notation
OOP	Object Oriented Programming
POJO	plain ol' JavaScript object
PR	pull request
PTC	Proper Tail Calls
TTI	Time to Interactive
UI	User Interface
URL	Uniform Resource Locator
XSS	cross-site scripting

PART I

A SKEPTIC'S GUIDE TO FUNCTIONAL PROGRAMMING WITH JAVASCRIPT

1

INTRODUCTION

There's something magical about functional programming. Again and again, I'm surprised and delighted by it. Somehow, applying this tiny set of constraints brings order out of chaos. And not just order, but safety. Somehow the code becomes more concise and yet *correct* at the same time. It's mysterious and, simultaneously, *solid*.

If you've tasted these delights, it's natural to want to share them. So we tell colleagues about it. Or we make posts to social media. Or throw up a pull request (PR) for comment. And it comes as quite the shock when people don't share our delight. Instead, they respond with criticism, suspicion, and outright disdain. It can be a crushing, discouraging experience.

If you've ever felt that disappointment, this book is for you.

This book is for people who already know a little about functional programming in JavaScript. In particular, it assumes you're comfortable with concepts like:

- Higher-order functions;
- Array comprehensions like `.map()`, `.filter()`, and `.reduce()`; and
- JavaScript's built-in function methods like `.bind()`, `.call()`, and `.apply()`.

It will also help if you've come across some algebraic structures before. That's things like monads, functors, applicatives, and the like. But it's not absolutely essential. If you're not familiar with those, don't worry. We'll explain them as we go along.

Speaking of explaining things, the book tries hard to explain things as we go, but there's only so much we can do. Hence, if you're new to coding in general, this book may not be the best place to start. You might want to take a look at *Free Code Camp*[1], *Codecademy*[2], or *JavaScript for Cats*[3]. We'll still be here when you come back.

If you're familiar with JavaScript, but not functional programming, you might be able to muddle along. There's plenty of help in the appendices. But if you find you're struggling, you may want to take a look at some of these excellent resources:

- *Professor Frisby's Mostly Adequate Guide to Functional Programming*[4];
- Reg Braithwaite's *JavaScript Allongé*[5];

---

[1] Free Code Camp: https://www.freecodecamp.org
[2] Codecademy: https://www.codecademy.com/learn/introduction-to-javascript
[3] JavaScript for Cats: http://jsforcats.com. In all seriousness, it's really good.
[4] Professor Frisby's Mostly Adequate Guide to Functional Programming: https://mostly-adequate.gitbook.io/mostly-adequate-guide/
[5] JavaScript Allongé: https://leanpub.com/javascriptallongesix/read

- Luis Atencio's *Functional Programming in JavaScript*[6];
- Kyle Simpson's *Functional-Light JavaScript*[7]; or
- My own motley collection of articles at
  `https://jrsinclair.com/web-development/`

And if you're a seasoned functional programmer and a JavaScript wizard, you may find some parts tedious. Some sections will explain things you already know. If you find yourself bored for this reason, please skip ahead. I promise I won't be offended.

§ 1.2. WHAT WILL YOU GET OUT OF THIS BOOK?

Over the years, I've come across a lot of myths and misinformation. Particularly when it comes to functional programming in JavaScript. This book aims to take a clear-eyed look at reality. Applying functional techniques to JavaScript can be frustrating sometimes. But it's not all bad, all the time. This book will help you sort out fact from fiction.

As we've hinted, functional programming in JavaScript isn't always easy. There are plenty of pitfalls and problem areas. In particular, JavaScript runtimes aren't great at optimising functional code. Hence, one of the most common criticisms you'll hear is that functional JavaScript is slow. This book will help you avoid the most common problems. Better yet, we'll look at how functional programming lets us apply performance optimisations with guaranteed safety.

At some point though, you'll find that pushback against functional programming isn't about the code. It has nothing to do with the technical merits of one approach versus another. The reasons

---

[6] Functional Programming in JavaScript: `https://www.manning.com/books/functional-programming-in-javascript`

[7] Functional-Light JavaScript: `https://github.com/getify/Functional-Light-JS`

why most people push back are cultural. They're about familiarity and comfort. About not wanting to look or feel stupid in front of others. So we'll also discuss how to have informed, reasonable conversations about these issues.

And in the end, it's important to remember why we're here in the first place. What's so great about functional programming anyway? If people are so critical, why do we even bother? Is it worth it? This book will help you articulate why functional programming produces better code. And in particular, it will help you be clear about what we mean by 'better'. Because if we don't really know why we're doing this, it's unlikely we'll ever convince anyone else.

§ 1.3. HOW THIS BOOK IS ORGANISED

You may be wondering about the chapter titles. Perhaps they seem a bit negative. Each chapter in this book represents a common complaint about functional programming in JavaScript. These complaints didn't come out of thin air. They're the result of hours and hours of researching online forums and Q&A sites to see what real people say about functional programming. These aren't the *only* problems, but they're the most common, based on my research.

The earlier chapters of the book, 2–5, focus mainly on practical issues. That is, they look at the technicalities of applying functional programming specifically in JavaScript. These include problems with the way JavaScript interpreters work, and how we organise code. Then in chapter 6, we shift perspective and look at JavaScript from the perspective of functional programmers outside the front-end community. And in chapter 7 we examine some of the more people-centric difficulties with functional programming, and why it's so hard for some people.

After the main body, I've included a number of appendices.

They are intended to help people out with background information in areas that might be a bit confusing. Many of these appendices have been adapted from blog posts on `jrsinclair.com`. If they seem familiar, that may be why.

WHAT'S SO GREAT ABOUT FUNCTIONAL PROGRAMMING ANYWAY?

To hear some people talk about functional programming, you'd think they'd joined some kind of cult. They prattle on about how it's changed the way they think about code. They'll extol the benefits of purity, at length. And proclaim that they are now able to "reason about their code"—as if all other code is irrational and incomprehensible. It's enough to make anyone skeptical.

Still, one has to wonder. There must be a reason these zealots are so excited. In my personal experience, it wasn't the lazy, incompetent programmers who developed an interest in functional programming.[1] Instead, the most intelligent coders I knew tended

---

[1] One of the people I showed this to had an interesting reaction. Their response was something like: "Hey! I like functional programming *because* I'm lazy and incompetent. It's about all the things I don't have to think about."

9

to take it up; the people most passionate about writing good code. (Though, they did tend towards the boffin end of the spectrum.) And this raises the question: What are they so excited about?

Faced with this question, most educators will start with the basics. They'll take you to the metaphorical baby pool. And they'll try to explain to you what functional programming *is*. They'll talk about "coding with expressions" and side effects, and purity, and ... they mean well. But telling people what functional programming *is* doesn't explain what functional programming is *good for.*

Lets' be honest. Nobody cares what functional programming *is*, at least, not at first. What we care about is, "can we deliver better code, faster?" And our project managers care about those in reverse order. Instead, let's try something different and skip the baby pool. Rather than talking about the definition of functional programming, we'll go straight to the good parts. Let's talk about Algebraic Structures.

§ 2.1. ALGEBRAIC STRUCTURES

Algebraic structures allow us to write expressive code, with more confidence. They're expressive because they convey a wealth of information. They tell us how code can be re-used, optimised, and rearranged. And all these with complete confidence we won't break anything. In some cases, they even enable automatic code generation.

These are bold claims. But by the end of this chapter, we will have demonstrated both:

- Reusable code; and
- Performance optimisation with guaranteed safety.

Furthermore, in later chapters, we'll show how algebraic structures allow our code to convey more information.

If they're so good, what are algebraic structures? In short, they're what lots of people consider the scary bits of functional programming. They include concepts like 'monoids', 'semigroups', 'functors', and the dreaded 'monad.' They're also super abstract—in the literal sense. Algebraic structures are abstractions of abstractions. In this way, they are a little bit like *design patterns*, such as those described in the 'gang of four' book *Design Patterns: Elements of Reusable Object-Oriented Software*.[2] But they have some significant differences too.

Once again though, instead of focussing on what they *are*, let's start with what they can do.

A REAL WORLD PROBLEM

If we want to see what functional programming (and algebraic structures) are good for, there's no point solving toy problems. We can do better than adding two numbers together. Instead, let's look at something JavaScript developers deal with often.

Let's imagine we're working on a web application. We have a list of notifications to display to the user. And we have them in an array of plain ol' JavaScript objects (POJOS). But, we need to transform them into a format that the front-end UI code can handle. Suppose the data looks something like this:

```
const notificationData = [
  {
    username: 'sherlock',
    message: 'Watson. Come at once if convenient.',
    date: -1461735479,
```

---

[2] Gamma et. al. (1994), *Design Patterns: Elements of Reusable Object-Oriented Software*, Addison-Wesley.

```
        displayName: 'Sherlock Holmes',
        id: 221,
        read: false,
        sourceId: 'note-to-watson-1895',
        sourceType: 'note',
    },
    {
        username: 'sherlock',
        message: 'If not convenient, come all the same.',
        date: -1461735359,
        displayName: 'Sherlock Holmes',
        id: 221,
        read: false,
        sourceId: 'note-to-watson-1895',
        sourceType: 'note',
    },
    // ... and so on. Imagine we had lots more entries here.
];
```

Now, to convert this data so our templating system can handle it, we need to do the following:

1. Generate a readable date;
2. Sanitise the message to prevent cross-site scripting (xss) attacks;
3. Build a link to the sender's profile page;
4. Build a link to the source of the notification; and
5. Tell the template what icon to display, based on the source type.

To get started, we write a function for each:[3]

---

[3] Please don't write your own xss sanitizing function. Use a battle-tested library, or let your view library (like React) take care of it. This is but an example for educational purposes.

```javascript
const getSet = (getKey, setKey, transform) => (obj) =>
({
  ...obj,
  [setKey]: transform(obj[getKey]),
});
const addReadableDate = getSet(
  'date',
  'readableDate',
  t => new Date(t * 1000).toGMTString()
);
const sanitizeMessage = getSet(
  'message',
  'message',
  msg => msg.replace(/</g, '&lt;')
);
const buildLinkToSender = getSet(
  'username',
  'sender',
  u => `https://example.com/users/${u}`
);


const buildLinkToSource = (notification) => ({
  ...notification,
  source: `https://example.com/${
    notification.sourceType
  }/${notification.sourceId}`
});
const urlPrefix = 'https://example.com/assets/icons/';
const iconSuffix = '-small.svg';
const addIcon = getSet(
```

```
  'sourceType',
  'icon',
  sourceType => `${urlPrefix}${sourceType}${iconSuffix}`
);
```

One way to wire all these together is to run them one-by-one, and store the results in named variables. For example:

```
const withDates = notificationData.map(addReadableDate);
const sanitized = withDates.map(sanitizeMessage);
const withSenders = sanitized.map(buildLinkToSender);
const withSources = withSenders.map(buildLinkToSource);
const dataForTemplate = withSources.map(addIcon);
```

Those interstitial variables don't add any new information, though. We can see what's going on from the name of the function we're mapping. Another way to wire it up would be to use some boring old JavaScript array method chaining. And as we do that, the code starts to look a little bit 'functional:'

```
const dataForTemplate = notificationData
  .map(addReadableDate)
  .map(sanitizeMessage)
  .map(buildLinkToSender)
  .map(buildLinkToSource)
  .map(addIcon);
```

Now, while this is truly 'functional' code, it's not overly special. Weren't we supposed to be talking about the wondrous benefits of algebraic structures?

Bear with me. We're going to rewrite this code using a couple of helper functions. The first is not complicated. We'll write a `map()`

function that, well, calls .map().[4]

```
const map = f => functor => functor.map(f);
```

Next, we write a pipe() function that lets us 'pipe' a value through a series of functions. It's a variation on function composition.[5]

```
const pipe = (x0, ...funcs) => funcs.reduce(
  (x, f) => f(x),
  x0
);
```

The pipe function uses the spread operator to turn all but the first argument into an array. Then it passes that first argument to the first function. And the result of that to the next function. And so on.

Now we can rewrite our transform code like so:

```
const dataForTemplate = pipe(
  notificationData,
  map(addReadableDate),
  map(sanitizeMessage),
  map(buildLinkToSender),
  map(buildLinkToSource),
  map(addIcon)
);
```

---

[4] If you're not used to seeing arrow functions that return arrow functions like that, check out the appendix on higher-order functions. We'll also explain this a bit more in Chapter 3 when we discuss currying.

[5] If you're not familiar with function composition, you can read more in the blog post *JavaScript function composition: What's the big deal?* https://jrsincla ir.com/articles/2022/javascript-function-composition-whats-the-big-deal/

The first thing to notice here, is that it looks a lot like the previous version using chained methods. But aside from that, it's still rather banal code. We can map over an array, so what? And worse still, it's inefficient.[6]

Hang in there. It's about to get more interesting.

§ 2.2. MAYBE

For the sake of argument, let's change the scenario a little. Instead of a list of notifications, suppose we've received the most recent one. But, we don't have complete confidence in our server. On occasion, something goes wrong, and it sends us an HTML page instead of JavaScript object notation (JSON) data. And we end up with undefined rather than a notification.

Now, one way to handle this would be to litter our code with if-statements. First, we catch the error, and return undefined if the response doesn't parse.

```
const parseJSON = (dataFromServer) => {
  try {
    const parsed = JSON.parse(dataFromServer);
    return parsed;
  } catch (_) {
    return undefined;
  }
};
```

Then we add if-statements to each of our utility functions.

---

[6] We'll come back to this in Chapter 4.

```
const addReadableDate = (notification) => {
  if (notification !== undefined) {
    return getSet(
      'date',
      'readableDate',
      t => new Date(t * 1000).toGMTString()
    )(notification);
  } else {
    return undefined;
  }
}

const sanitizeMessage = (notification) => {
  if (notification !== undefined) {
    return getSet(
      'message',
      'message',
      msg => msg.replace(/</g, '&lt;')
    )(notification)
  } else {
    return undefined;
  }
};

const buildLinkToSender = (notification) => {
  if (notification !== undefined) {
    return getSet(
      'username',
      'sender',
      u => `https://example.com/users/${u}`
    );
  } else {
```

```
    return undefined;
  }
};
const buildLinkToSource = (notification) => {
  if (notification !== undefined) {
    return ({
      ...notification,
      source: `https://example.com/${
        notification.sourceType
      }/${notification.sourceId}`
    });
  } else {
    return undefined;
  }
};
const urlPrefix = 'https://example.com/assets/icons/';
const iconSuffix = '-small.svg';
const addIcon = (notification) => {
  if (notification !== undefined) {
    return getSet(
      'sourceType',
      'icon',
      (sourceType) =>
        `${urlPrefix}${sourceType}${iconSuffix}`
    )(notification);
  } else {
    return undefined;
  }
};
```

After all that, our main `pipe()` call still looks the same.

```
const dataForTemplate = pipe(
  notificationData,
  map(addReadableDate),
  map(sanitizeMessage),
  map(buildLinkToSender),
  map(buildLinkToSource),
  map(addIcon)
);
```

But, as you can see, it makes our individual functions verbose and repetitive. Surely there must be an alternative? And indeed, there is. We'll write a pair of functions like so:

```
const Just = (val) => ({
  map: f => Just(f(val)),
});
```

```
const Nothing = () => {
  const nothing = { map: () => nothing };
  return nothing;
};
```

Both Just and Nothing return an object with a .map() method. When used together, we call this pair a Maybe. And we use it like so:

```
const parseJSON = (data) => {
  try {
    return Just(JSON.parse(data));
  } catch (_) {
    return Nothing();
```

```
  }
}
const notificationData = parseJSON(dataFromServer);
```

With that in place, let's look at our mapping code. In this new
scenario, we're no longer working with arrays. Instead, we have a
single value that may be Nothing. Or, it may be Just a notification.
But, as a reminder, here's the code we had for arrays again:

```
const dataForTemplate = pipe(
  notificationData,
  map(addReadableDate),
  map(sanitizeMessage),
  map(buildLinkToSender),
  map(buildLinkToSource),
  map(addIcon)
);
```

What do we need to make this work with Maybe a single value?
Almost nothing. All we need is a way to get our value out of the
Just wrapper at the end. To do that, we'll add another method to
Just and Nothing.

```
const Just = (val) => ({
  map: f => Just(f(val)),
  reduce: (f, x0) => f(x0, val),
});

const Nothing = () => {
  const nothing = {
    map: () => nothing,
```

```
    reduce: (_, x0) => x0,
  };
  return nothing;
};
```

Notice how we've added reduce() to both Just and Nothing. That allows us write a stand-alone reduce() function, much like we did for map():

```
const reduce = (f, x0) => foldable =>
    foldable.reduce(f, x0);
```

If we want to get our value out of a Just, we can call reduce() like so:

```
reduce((_, val) => val, fallbackValue);
```

If reduce() encounters Nothing, it will return the fallback value. Otherwise, it will ignore fallback value and returns the data.

So the pipeline would look like so:

```
const dataForTemplate = pipe(
  notificationData,
  map(addReadableDate),
  map(sanitizeMessage),
  map(buildLinkToSender),
  map(buildLinkToSource),
  map(addIcon),
  reduce((_, val) => val, fallbackValue),
);
```

Now, you may be wondering, why all this rigmarole with .re-
duce()? Why not add a method that provides the fallback value
straight away? For example:

```
const Just = (val) => ({
  map: f => Just(f(val)),
  fallbackTo: (_) => val,
});

const Nothing = () => {
  const nothing = {
    map: () => nothing,
    fallBackTo: (x0) => x0,
  };
  return nothing;
};
```

Once again, because we've added .fallBackTo() to both, we
can write another utility function. This will work regardless of
whether we get Just or Nothing. It will do what we expect either
way.

```
const fallBackTo = (x0) => (m) => m.fallBackTo(x0);
```

This utility function, fallBackTo() is concise and effective.
Why bother with reduce()?

It's a good question. At first glance, it appears to be the kind of
needlessly complicated code that makes functional programmers
so annoying. Always adding in layers of abstraction that make code
harder to read, and confusing for juniors. Right?

There's a good reason for using reduce() instead of fall-
BackTo(), though. Because reduce() can work with other data

structures besides Just and Nothing. It's portable code. The truth is, for this code, we can replace Just and Nothing with something else. What would happen if we rewrote the parsing code like this:

```
const parseJSON = strData => {
  try { return [JSON.parse(strData)]; }
  catch () { return []; }
};


const notificationData = parseJSON(dataFromServer);
```

Instead of using Just and Nothing, we're now returning plain ol' JavaScript arrays. If we look at our pipeline again:

```
const dataForTemplate = pipe(
  notificationData,
  map(addReadableDate),
  map(sanitizeMessage),
  map(buildLinkToSender),
  map(buildLinkToSource),
  map(addIcon),
  reduce((_, val) => val, fallbackValue),
);
```

We don't change a single line. But it still produces the same result.

§ 2.3. RESULT

Let's stick with this scenario a moment longer. In our JSON parsing code, we ignore the error in the catch clause. But, what if that error has useful information inside? We may want to log the error somewhere so we can debug issues.

Let's go back to our old Just/Nothing code. We'll switch out Nothing for a slightly different function, Err. And while we're at it, we'll also rename Just to OK.

```
const OK = (val) => ({
  map:  (f) => OK(f(val)),
  reduce: (f, x0) => f(x0, val),
});

const Err = (e) => ({
  const err = {
    map: (_) => err,
    reduce: (_, x0) => x0,
  };
  return err;
});
```

We'll call this new pair of functions, Result.[7] With that in place, we can change our parseJSON() code so that it uses Result.

```
const parseJSON = strData => {
  try { return OK(JSON.parse(strData)); }
  catch (e) { return Err(e); }
}

const notificationData = parseJSON(dataFromServer);
```

Now, instead of ignoring the error, we capture it in an Err object. If we go back to the pipeline, we don't have to change anything. Since Err has compatible .map() and .reduce() methods, it still

---

[7] You'll find functional libraries often offer a similar structure called 'Either'.

works.

```
const dataForTemplate = pipe(
  notificationData,
  map(addReadableDate),
  map(sanitizeMessage),
  map(buildLinkToSender),
  map(buildLinkToSource),
  map(addIcon),
  reduce((_, val) => val, fallbackValue),
);
```

Of course, we're still ignoring the error when we get to that final reduce(). To fix that, we need to make a firm decision about what we want to do with that error. Do we want to log it to the console, introducing a side-effect? Do we want to send it over the network to a logging platform? Or do we want to extract something from it and display it to the user?

For now, let's assume we're OK with a small side effect, and we'll log it to the console. We add a .peekErr() method to both OK and Err like so:

```
const OK = (val) => ({
  map: (f) => OK(f(val)),
  reduce: (f, x0) => f(x0, val),
  peekErr: () => OK(val),
});

const Err = (e) => ({
  const err = {
    map: (_) => err,
```

```
    reduce: (_, x0) => x0,
    peekErr: (f) => { f(x); return err; }
  }
  return err;
});
```

The version we add to OK does nothing, because there's no error to peek at. But having it there allows us to write a utility function that works with both OK and Err.

```
const peekErr = (f) => (result) => result.peekErr(f);
```

Then we can add peekErr() to our pipeline:

```
const dataForTemplate = pipe(
  notificationData,
  map(addReadableDate),
  map(sanitizeMessage),
  map(buildLinkToSender),
  map(buildLinkToSource),
  map(addIcon),
  peekErr(console.warn),
  reduce((_, val) => val, fallbackValue),
);
```

If there happens to be an error, we log it and move on. If we needed more complex error handling, we might use other structures.

Of course, adding peekErr() breaks compatibility with Arrays and the Maybe structure. And that's fine. Arrays and Maybe don't have this extra error data to deal with.

Now, this is all well and good, but we've been ignoring something important. All along we've been saying that this data comes from a server. But retrieving data from a server implies that there's some sort of network call involved. And in JavaScript, that most often means asynchronous code.

For example, suppose we have some code that fetches our notification data using standard JavaScript promises:

```
const notificationDataPromise = fetch(urlForData)
  .then(response => response.json());
```

Let's see if we can build a structure that works for asynchronous code too. To do this, we're going to create a structure with a constructor function much like a Promise. It expects a function that takes two arguments:

1. One to call on successful resolution; and
2. Another to call if something goes wrong.

We can call it like so:

```
const notificationData = Task((resolve, reject) =>
    fetch(urlForData)
        .then(response => response.json())
        .then(resolve)
        .catch(reject)
);
```

In this example, we call fetch and pass it the URL for our notification. Then we call .json() on the response to parse the data. And with that done, we resolve() if the call was successful, or reject()

if it wasn't. It looks a little awkward compared to the Promise-only `fetch()` code. But that's so we can wire up the resolve and reject. We'll add a helper for wiring up asynchronous functions like `fetch()` in a moment.

The implementation for our `Task` structure is not too complex:

```
const Task = (run) => ({
  map: (f) => Task((resolve, reject) => {
    run(
      (x) => (resolve(f(x))),
      reject
    );
  }),
  peekErr: (f) => Task((resolve, reject) => {
    run(
      resolve,
      (err) => { f(err); reject(err); }
    )
  }),
  run: (onResolve, onReject) => run(
    onResolve,
    onReject
  ),
});
```

We have `.map()` and `.peekErr()`, as we did for Result. But a `.reduce()` method doesn't make sense for asynchronous code. Once you go asynchronous, you can never go back. We've also added a `.run()` method to kick off our Task.

To make working with Promises a little easier, we can add a static helper to `Task`. And another helper for fetching JSON data:

```
Task.fromAsync = (asyncFunc) => (...args) =>
  Task((resolve, reject) => {
    asyncFunc(...args).then(resolve).catch(reject);
  });

const taskFetchJSON = Task.fromAsync(
  (url) => fetch(url).then(data => data.json())
);
```

With those helpers, we can define notificationData like so:

```
const notificationData = taskFetchJSON(urlForData);
```

To work with Task, we need to change our pipeline a little. But it's a small change:

```
const dataForTemplate = pipe(
  notificationData,
  map(addReadableDate),
  map(sanitizeMessage),
  map(buildLinkToSender),
  map(buildLinkToSource),
  map(addIcon),
  peekErr(console.warn),
);
```

Most of it still works, except for the reduce() function. But we still want some way to introduce a fallback value if the network request or parsing fails. To make that happen, we'll add a method called .scan(). It will be like .reduce(), but we give it a different name to acknowledge that the result will still be 'inside' a Task.

```
const Task = (run) => ({
  map: (f) => Task((resolve, reject) => {
    run(
      (x) => (resolve(f(x))),
      reject
    );
  }),
  peekErr: (f) => Task((resolve, reject) => {
    run(
      resolve,
      (err) => { f(err); reject(err); }
    )
  }),
  run: (onResolve, onReject) => run(
      onResolve,
      onReject
    );
  scan: (f, x0) => Task((resolve, reject) => run(
    x => resolve(f(x0, x)),
    e => resolve(x0),
  )),
});
```

Notice that .scan() doesn't call reject(). This is because it's analogous to .reduce(). It lets us fall back to a default value if we have an error.

And, as usual, we'll create a matching utility function:

```
const scan = (f, x0) => (scannable) =>
  scannable.scan(f, x0);
```

With that in place, we can adjust our pipeline like so:

```
const taskForTemplateData = pipe(
  notificationData,
  map(addReadableDate),
  map(sanitizeMessage),
  map(buildLinkToSender),
  map(buildLinkToSource),
  map(addIcon),
  peekErr(console.warn),
  scan((_, val) => val, fallback)
);
```

And to run it, we do something like this:

```
taskForTemplateData.run(
  renderNotifications,
  handleError
);
```

WHY NOT USE PROMISES?

Someone might be wondering, JavaScript already has a built-in data structure for asynchronous code. Why not use Promises? Why bother with this Task business? What's the point, if it's going to confuse everyone?

There's at least three reasons. The first is that Promises don't have a .run() method. This means they kick off as soon as you create them. Using Task gives us precise control over when everything starts.

Now, we don't *need* Task to get this control. If we want to, we can delay our Promises by putting them inside a function. Then, the Promise won't 'kick off' until we call the function. Along the way though, we've as-good-as reinvented Task. But with a different syntax and less flexibility.

The second reason for preferring Task is it has abilities Promises don't. The main one is being able to nest Tasks. We can run a Task, and get back another Task. We can then wait and decide when to run that next Task. This isn't possible with Promises.[8] Promises smoosh `.map()` and `.flatMap()` together into a single `.then()` method. And as a consequence, we lose flexibility (again).

The final reason for preferring Task is that it's consistent with other algebraic structures. If we keep using these structures often enough, they become familiar. And in turn, it becomes easier to make inferences about what the code is doing. Or (more importantly) *not* doing. We'll discuss this further in a moment.

In summary, Task gives us more power, flexibility, and consistency. This isn't to say that there's no tradeoffs using tasks. With the `async ... await` keywords, JavaScript supports Promises 'out of the box'. We may not want to give up that convenience to use Tasks. And that's okay.

§ 2.5. SO YOU USED POLYMORPHISM. BIG DEAL.

We started this chapter asking the question "What's so great about functional programming?" But all we've done so far is talk about a handful of objects that share some method names. That's plain old polymorphism. Object Oriented Programming (OOP) gurus have been banging on about polymorphism for decades. We can't claim that functional programming is awesome because it uses polymorphism.

Or can we?

---

[8] At least, it's impossible with Promises, unless you return a function that returns a Promise. But, as discussed, a function that returns a Promise is another way of constructing a Task.

It's not polymorphism itself that makes algebraic structures (and functional programming) so awesome. But polymorphism makes algebraic structures possible in JavaScript. In our notifications example, we defined some methods with matching names and signatures. For example, `.map()` and `.reduce()`. Then we wrote utility functions that work with methods matching those signatures, for example, `map()` and `reduce()`. Polymorphism makes those utility functions work.

Those method definitions (and utility functions) aren't arbitrary. They're not design patterns that someone made up by observing common architectural patterns. No, algebraic structures come from mathematics; from fields like set theory and category theory. This means that, as well as specific method signatures, these structures come with *laws*.

At first, this doesn't sound wonderful. We associate mathematics with confusion and boredom. And we associate laws with restriction. Laws get in our way. They stop us doing what we want. They're inconvenient. But if you take a moment to read these laws, they may surprise you. Because they're *boring*. Incredibly boring.

Now, you may be thinking "I'm not sure why you thought that would be surprising. That's the least surprising thing ever." But these laws are a particular kind of boring. They're boring in the sense that they state the obvious. The kind of thing where you wonder why anyone bothered to write it down. We read them and tend to think "Of course it works like that. In what scenario would it ever be different?" And that, there, is the beauty of algebraic structures.

To illustrate, let's look back at our notifications example. We've made use of at least two algebraic structures. One of them, we call Functor. All that means is that in Maybe, Result, and Task, we wrote a `.map()` method. And the way we've written those `.map()` methods, each one follows some laws. We also used another algebraic structure called Foldable. We call a data structure Foldable if it has a `.reduce()` method, and that method obeys some laws.

One of the laws for Functor says that the following two pieces of code must always produce the same result. No matter what. Assuming we have two pure functions, f, and g, our first piece of code is:

```
const resultA = a.map(f).map(g);
```

And the second piece of code is:

```
const resultB = a.map(x => g(f(x)));
```

These two pieces of code must produce the same result when given the same input. That is, resultA ≡ resultB. We call this the composition rule. And we can apply it to our pipeline code. Because x => g(f(x)) is the same as writing x => pipe(x, f, g). That is, our pipe() function is a form of composition. Thus, if we go all the way back to the array-based version of our pipeline, we have:

```
const dataForTemplate = pipe(
  notificationData,
  map(addReadableDate),
  map(sanitizeMessage),
  map(buildLinkToSender),
  map(buildLinkToSource),
  map(addIcon),
);
```

We can rewrite it as:

```
const dataForTemplate = map(x => pipe(x,
  addReadableDate,
  sanitizeMessage,
  buildLinkToSender,
  buildLinkToSource,
  addIcon,
))(notificationData);
```

Because of the composition law, we know these two pieces of code are equivalent. It doesn't matter if we're working with a Maybe, Result, Task, or an Array. These two pieces of code will always produce the same result.

Now, it's possible, that doesn't look like a big deal to you. And you may even think the second version is uglier, and overly complex. But for arrays, that second version will be more efficient. The first version will produce at least five intermediate arrays as it passes data through the pipe. The second version does it all in one pass. We get a performance improvement that's guaranteed to produce the same result as the code we started with. Well, guaranteed, so long as we're using pure functions.

§ 2.6. SO WHAT?

It's all about confidence. Those laws tell me that if I use an algebraic structure, it will behave as I expect. And I have a mathematical guarantee that it will continue to do so. 100%. All the time.

As promised, we've demonstrated code that we can re-use. Our utility functions like map(), reduce() and pipe() work with a bunch of different structures. Structures like Array, Maybe, Either, and Task. And we showed how the laws of algebraic structures helped us rearrange the code with complete safety.

And showed how that rearrangement provided a performance improvement. Again, with complete confidence.

This, in turn, gets to the heart of what's great about functional programming. It's not mainly about algebraic structures. They're but one set of tools in a gigantic tool chest. Functional programming is all about having confidence in our code. It's about knowing that our code is doing what we expect, and *nothing but* what we expect.

Once we understand this, the eccentricities of functional programming start to make a little more sense. This is why, for example, functional programmers are so careful about side-effects. The more we work with pure functions, the more certainty we gain. It also explains the love affair some programmers have with fancy type systems like the one in Haskell.[9] They're addicted to the drug of certainty.

This knowledge—that functional programming is about confidence in your code—is like having a secret key. It explains why functional programmers get all worked up about ostensibly trivial matters. It's not that they enjoy pedantry. (Well, okay, *some* of them appear to enjoy pedantry a lot). Most of the time, they're fighting to preserve confidence. And they're willing to do whatever it takes. Even if it involves delving into the dark arts of mathematics.

---

[9] To be clear, not all functional programmers end up besotted with fancy type systems.

FUNCTIONAL PROGRAMMING MAKES JAVASCRIPT UNREADABLE

A common criticism of functional programming is that it turns your JavaScript code into an unreadable, unmaintainable mess. At least, it will if you take it too far. Functional code may be fine for the odd data pipeline, but any more, and it will harm your code. Or, so the argument goes.

Now, it's important to recognise that these objections come up for a reason. They're born of real-life frustrations. Here's a scenario to consider: An experienced developer has a team member who learns a new functional programming technique. And said team member becomes a little ... *enthusiastic* about it. The enthusiast then proceeds to over-apply this technique and causes trouble for the rest of the team. Or even themselves. Either way, the result is, functional programming gets the blame.

There's at least three common causes for these kinds of scenario:

1. Over-application of currying;
2. Over-application of point-free style; and
3. Overly 'concise' code—sometimes described as code golf.

We'll look at each one in turn, starting with currying.

§ 3.1. CURRYING

If you're already familiar with currying and partial application, feel free to skip ahead.

What is currying? In short, it's a way of changing how arguments get applied to a function. It's related to partial application. And the two concepts are often conflated.

PARTIAL APPLICATION

Partial application is what we do when we take a function that expects more than one argument and transform it into a function that expects fewer arguments. We do this by 'fixing' one of the arguments to a specific value.

For example, imagine we have a function called hTag():

```
const hTag = (tag, body) => `<${tag}>
  ${body}
</${tag}>`;
```

If we want to, we can partially apply the tag argument to create functions for different HTML elements. For example:

```
const h1 = (body) => hTag('h1', body);
const strong = (body) => hTag('strong', body);
```

Here, we've taken one function hTag(), and specialised it. By
partially applying the first parameter, we've created two new functions. Each with a more specific purpose. And using the specific
function conveys a bit more information about what we're doing.
Calling strong(), as opposed to hTag(), gives a clearer signal about
our intent.

We can do this partial application trick for any number of parameters. For example, imagine we expanded our hTag() function
into a more flexible el() function. It takes three arguments:

```
const el = (tag, attrs, body) =>
`<${tag} ${Object.entries(attrs).map(([k, v]) =>
  `${k}="${v}"`).join("\n")}>
  ${body}
</${tag}>`;
```

Using partial application, we can, for example, create a function
specifically for anchor links:

```
const a = (attrs, body) => el('a', attrs, body);
```

We can also fix more than one argument. For example, we can
create a function for creating home links:

```
const homeLink = (body) => el('a', {
  class: 'home',
  href: '/',
}, body);
```

Currying is related to partial application, but isn't the same thing. With currying we don't fix any arguments. Instead, currying converts a function that takes two or more arguments into a series of functions that each take one argument.

For example, we can curry our hTag() and el() functions like so:

```
curriedHTag = tag => body => hTag(tag, body);
curriedEl = tag => attrs => body => el(tag, attrs, body);
```

This is convenient if we want to create partially applied functions:

```
const h1 = curriedHTag('h1');
const strong = curriedHTag('strong');
const a = curriedEl('a');
const homeLink = a({class: 'home', href: '/'});
```

It looks unusual if we call a curried function all at once. But it works all the same:

```
const homeProps = {class: 'home', href: '/'};
const homeLink = curriedEl('a')(homeProps)('home');
const strongWord = curriedHTag('strong')('word');
```

WHY WOULD YOU DO THIS?

Lots of people find this way of calling functions strange. In particular, it can be difficult to get used to the idea of functions frequently returning other functions. Most people feel comfortable with the idea of this happening every now and then, in 'special' circumstances. But the idea that we would see this in everyday code causes some people difficulty. We're not used to treating functions as values.

Which raises the question, why would you bother with currying at all? If you think about it, partial application makes some sense. We often find ourselves situations where we need a function that fits a particular shape (that is, a type signature). And we use partial application to munge another function into the shape we need. For example, composing functions with `pipe()` requires each function in the pipeline to take precisely one input. If we have a function that takes more inputs, we use partial application to pare it down to one.

The more we work with higher-order functions, the more this comes up. Functions like `map()` and `reduce()` work with functions of a specific arity.[1] And partial application is the magic tool that helps us wire everything together.

Currying takes this a step further, and turns any function into a single parameter function. And the advantage here is that it makes our JavaScript functions more like mathematical functions. That, in turn, allows us to apply mathematical laws and tricks to them. And if we're doing a whole bunch of partial application anyway, it's convenient.

AUTOCURRYING

In languages like Elm and Haskell, currying is default behaviour. In JavaScript though, currying functions takes more effort. But JavaScript is a flexible language. It's possible to write a utility function to help with currying. It takes a function of arbitrary arity and returns a curried version.

---

[1] 'Arity' is a fancy word for the number of parameters a function expects.

```
const autocurry = f => {
  const arity = f.length;
  const given = argsSoFar => {
    const helper = (...args) => {
      const newArgsSoFar = argsSoFar.concat(args);
      return (newArgsSoFar.length >= arity)
        ? f(...newArgsSoFar)
        : given(newArgsSoFar)
    };
    return helper;
  };
  return given([]);
};
```

This utility is interesting because it does a little more than what currying by hand does. We can call an 'autocurried' function in a variety of ways. For example:

```
const curriedEl = autocurry(el);
const h1a = curriedEl('h1')({})('Title');
const h1b = curriedEl('h1', {})('Title');
const h1c = curriedEl('h1')({}, 'Title');
const h1d = curriedEl('h1', {}, 'Title');

(h1a === h1b) && (h1a === h1c) && (h1a === h1d) // true
```

In the functional programming world, this autocurrying is a bit strange. It's strange in that stricter languages like PureScript or Haskell don't work like this. It doesn't make sense, because everything is always curried. But those languages also provide syntax that makes calling curried function convenient. We don't have that in JavaScript, so autocurrying gives us flexibility. We can apply more than one parameter at a time, without lots of parentheses.

THE TROUBLE WITH AUTOCURRY

Some people love the flexibility autocurry provides. The Ramda library, for example, curries every function this way. And it does make it convenient to use these functions with function combinators.[2] But not everyone loves it.

Some criticise this form of currying because it has drawbacks:

1. Autocurrying introduces a lot of ambiguity into the code. With autocurried functions it can be easy to lose track of whether you're getting a function or a value back for any particular call.

2. This ambiguity is exacerbated by the 'trickiness' of the `curry()` function. That is, it's difficult to give this function a correct type in TypeScript or Flow. And this causes other problems as any types start to creep into the codebase.

3. Even if we don't care about TypeScript or Flow, we still lose the ability to use default parameters.

For these reasons, even some functional programming enthusiasts tend to avoid autocurry. Instead, they often prefer to curry manually. Manual currying is much more convenient than it used to be, now that we have arrow functions in JavaScript. And if we can't be bothered to curry our functions by hand, we can write a strict currying function like so:

```
const strictCurry = f => {
  const arity = f.length;
  const given = argsSoFar => {
```

---

[2] For more on function combinators, see https://gist.github.com/Avaq/1f0636e c5c8d6aed2e45.

```
      const helper = (arg) => {
        const newArgsSoFar = argsSoFar.concat([arg]);
        return (newArgsSoFar.length >= arity)
          ? f(...newArgsSoFar)
          : given(newArgsSoFar)
      };
      return helper;
    };
    return given([]);
  };
```

With this version of currying, we have to supply each argument, one at a time. And each argument gets its own parentheses. But, this reduces the ambiguity introduced by autocurry. And further, it eliminates most of the type signature difficulties.

THE TROUBLE WITH CURRY

Even if we stick with strict currying, people still object to currying as a practice. Often, people can't see the point. Why bother with currying? And, to be fair, if you write in a procedural style most of the time, currying isn't much use. Furthermore, currying has other disadvantages:

1. It sometimes introduces a bunch of 'unnecessary' parentheses to the code.
2. Using currying forces you to consider that every return value might be a function. People often find it difficult to unlearn the expectation that functions (almost) always return plain values.
3. Currying introduces unfamiliar patterns, so it takes less experienced readers longer to comprehend.

As we mentioned, though, the more we work with higher-order

functions, the more useful currying becomes. If you'll forgive the whacky metaphor, currying is like Power Coin that transforms an ordinary teenager into a *Mighty Morhphin' Power Ranger*. And this power coin allows them to pilot the powerful *Dinozords*.[3] Now, every episode of the *Power Rangers* culminates in the Dinozords facing a powerful foe. One too powerful for them to defeat individually. Faced with a challenge of this size, the Dinozords combine to become a mighty Megazord. And this giant humanoid robot will smite its enemies with an arsenal of lethal weaponry.

In a similar way, currying a pure function gives that function superpowers. Ordinarily, functions can only compose if they're unary. That is, if they take a single argument. But currying transforms a multivariate function into an unary function. This places it in the realm of mathematical functions. Harnessing the power of composition, our super-curried-function can combine with other functions. And together, they form powerful applications—much like a Megazord.

Now, yes, that's a cheesy metaphor. But the point is, currying serves a useful purpose. It enables a host of other tools, tricks, and techniques. And one of those is a style of programming called 'point free'.

§ 3.2. POINT-FREE STYLE

Once again, if you're already familiar with point-free code, feel free to skip ahead.

'Point-free' is another technique that people blame for making code unreadable. It's a style of coding where we build functions out of other functions, using nothing but composition. As a consequence, with this style, we never need to name any function param-

---

[3] https://en.m.wikipedia.org/wiki/Mighty_Morphin_Power_Rangers

eters or variables. Functions get names, but nothing else does.

WHY GO POINT-FREE?

Why would anyone want to twist their code such that there's no data variables? It seems like an odd thing to do. To understand why it might appeal, lets' revisit the pipeline example from last chapter:

```
const tplData = pipe(
  notificationData,
  map(addReadableDate),
  map(sanitizeMessage),
  map(buildLinkToSender),
  map(buildLinkToSource),
  map(addIcon),
  reduce((_, val) => val, fallbackValue),
);
```

This pipeline, as written, is *almost* point-free. We pass data from map(sanitizeMessage), to map(buildLinkToSender), and then to map(buildLinkToSource), and so on. We do this without ever naming the interstitial objects. If we were to write this without the help of pipe(), though, it might look like so:

```
const withDate = notificationData.map(addReadableDate);
const sanitized = withDate.map(sanitizeMessage);
const withSender = sanitized.map(buildLinkToSender);
const withSource = withSender.map(buildLinkToSource);
const withIcon = withSource.map(addIcon);
const tplData = withIcon.reduce(
  (_, val) => val,
```

```
    fallbackValue
);
```

Now, some people may find this version easier to understand. And they may find it easier to read too. We'll discuss this further in Section 3.6. For now, regardless of how readable the code is, we're duplicating information. For example, we name a variable with-Date straight after we call .map(addReadableDate). This doesn't add any new information. It's redundant. What's more, we create a variable for every single operation. Which means we have to invent a name for each of these variables. And this is a bigger deal than it sounds. Naming things is *hard*. And here, we name a lot of variables, only to use them once and throw them away.

The version we wrote with pipe() conveys all the same information. But it does so with a lot less noise. There's less focus on *how* to get the job done, and more on *what* we're trying to do. That is, it's more declarative.

HOW DO WE GO POINT-FREE, THEN?

If we were to make our pipeline truly point-free, we'd need to change the reduce() call at the end. And we also need to switch out pipe() for another composition function, flow(). Using pipe() for point-free style doesn't work because it expects a value as the first argument. The flow() function though, does not. It works like this:

```
const flow = (...fns) => x0 => fns.reduce(
  (f, x) => f(x),
  x0
);
```

With that in place, we can now create a processNotifica-
tions() function:

```
const processNotifications = flow(
  map(readableDate),
  map(sanitizeMessage),
  map(buildLinkToSender),
  map(buildLinkToSource),
  map(addIcon),
  reduce((_, val) => val, fallback)
);
```

And we would use our new function like so:

```
const tplData = processNotifications(notificationData);
```

Notice that there's no function body for processNotifica-
tions(). We've built it as a series of composed functions. But it's
not entirely point-free yet, as we still have that tricky reduce()
bit at the end.

To make it truly point-free, we need a helper function for the
reducer. And we also need to rearrange the order that reduce()
takes its arguments.

The helper function is rather short:

```
const secondArg = (_, val) => val;
```

And the rearranged version of reduce() looks like this:

```
const curriedReduce = reducerFn => x0 => mx =>
  mx.reduce(reducerFn, x0);
```

So now, our processNotifications() function looks like so:

```
const processNotifications = flow(
  map(readableDate),
  map(sanitizeMessage),
  map(buildLinkToSender),
  map(buildLinkToSource),
  map(addIcon),
  curriedReduce(secondArg)
);
```

Before, processNotifications() was a function that took a notifications functor (like an array) and returned another notifications functor (of the same type). But we've changed that. Now, processNotifications() takes a functor of notifications and returns a new function. This new function takes a fallback value, and returns yet another function. This final function takes a notifications functor and returns a new a notification functor. In other words, it now takes an extra, curried, parameter:

```
const tplData =
    processNotifications(fallback)(notifications);
```

WEIGHING UP POINT-FREE CODE

You can see why some people get riled up about point-free style in JavaScript. Because we've lost information. Unless we're using TypeScript or Flow, it's difficult to tell that processNotifications is a curried function needing two arguments. To let other developers know what's going on, we'd need to annotate it with comments. And so, we can understand why some people argue that point-free code makes JavaScript 'unreadable.'

Except, it's not the point-free style that's at fault here. It's over-enthusisatic application of a technique where it doesn't make sense.

You see, it's theoretically possible to make any piece of code point-free. (Assuming it's pure.) In theory, we can convert any operator into a function. And we can curry any multi-argument function in to a series of single argument functions. And if we have single argument functions, then we can apply an algorithm, called eta-reduction, to remove any mention of arguments. In theory, it's possible.

That doesn't mean it's a good idea though.

I've never come across a single functional programmer that recommends everyone go all-in on point-free code. In other places, I've sometimes suggested it's worth trying as a learning exercise on a small project. But I've always been careful to specify that it's wise do this on a solo project. Never when you're working with other people. And even the Haskellers I've met who love point-free style will admit that it's an acquired taste. It's not for everyone.

§ 3.3. READABILITY, FAMILIARITY, AND EXPRESSIVITY.

Let's look at our working example again. If we relax a little and absolve ourselves of absolute adherence to point-free style, our code can be rather expressive. All the more so if we put a wrapper around the final reduce().

```
const fallbackOnEmpty = fallbackVal => mx =>
  mx.reduce((_, x) => x, fallbackVal);
```

With that in place, our main flow looks like so:

```
const processNotifications = flow(
  map(readableDate),
```

```
map(sanitizeMessage),
map(buildLinkToSender),
map(buildLinkToSource),
map(addIcon),
fallbackOnEmpty(fallback)
);
```

Now, to me, this code is readable. It's clear that this function performs a series of map operations. That implies it's expecting a functor. And fallbackOnEmpty() is reasonably descriptive. It's all readable, *to me*, because I'm familiar with flow() as a away of composing functions. I'm familiar with functors being a thing you can map() over. And I'm also familiar with the idea that reduce() folds structures into single values. Thus, to me, all this is clear and readable. Because I'm *familiar* with these algebraic structures.

Not everyone finds this code readable, though. Because not everyone is familiar with higher-order functions and algebraic structures like Functor and Foldable. Some people have built up a set of assumptions as they've read and written JavaScript code for years. And this style of code may break those assumptions.

In particular, they may assume that functions returning functions in JavaScript is a rare and special event. Something done in times of great need or to solve a tricky problem. But this code has functions returning functions on every line. It doesn't fit their expectations of what 'readable' JavaScript code looks like. Perhaps they're used to other languages where returning a function *is* a rare and special event. Or perhaps in the languages they're used to working with, returning a function isn't even possible. Either way, it's unfamiliar and unexpected. Hence they declare code like this 'unreadable.'

The trouble is, they're correct. To them, this code is unreadable.

While for you and me, it may be easy to read. Which one is it? Is this code readable or not? Whose opinion is correct?

The answer is, everyone's. We're all correct. Because readability is subjective. It depends on how familiar the reader is with the code in use. And unless we recognise that, we'll waste a lot of time in pointless arguments.

§ 3.4. FREEDOM OF EXPRESSION

It's still possible to have a reasonable discussion though. That is, so long as we're clear what we're talking about. The function pipeline from our example may not be readable for *everyone*, but it's expressive. If you're familiar with Functor and Foldable, our pipeline packs a lot of information into a small space.

Let's look at it again, this time with `.reduce()` back in:

```
const processNotifications = flow(
  map(readableDate),
  map(sanitizeMessage),
  map(buildLinkToSender),
  map(buildLinkToSource),
  map(addIcon),
  reduce((_, val) => val, fallback)
);
```

Here's a handful of facts we can gather from this code, at a glance:

- If we pass an array into this pipeline, each `map()` operation will return an array of the same length. This is because map operations preserve the structure of the Functor they're working on.
- Since the pipeline uses `map()` and `reduce()` without any array-

specific functions, this code can work on any Foldable Functor. That is, so long as we're obeying the laws for those structures.

- The reduce() at the end tells us we may not have a functor at the end, since we're folding it into another type.
- The functor laws tell us that we could swap the series of map() operations at the start for single map() of composed functions. And we can make this swap with a guarantee that the output will be the same (assuming pure functions). We saw this in Chapter 2.
- The flow() pipeline tells us how each function in the argument list relates to the others. We know, for example, that map(addIcon) expects as input the type of data that map(buildLinkToSource) outputs. And, by implication (the composition law again), addIcon() expects the kind of data that buildLinkToSource() outputs.

That's a lot of information packed into a small amount of space. But the point here is not about how concise the code is. Rather, it's about the signal-to-noise ratio. Regardless of how readable you find it, this code is efficient communication. It focuses like a laser on *what* this code is doing. And it hides away the details of *how* it gets that done. That makes this code more declarative, and more expressive.

Speaking of the details though, let's take another look at the pipeline functions:

```
const getSet = (getKey, setKey, transform)
  => (obj) => ({
    ...obj,
    [setKey]: transform(obj[getKey]),
  });

const addReadableDate = getSet(
  'date',
```

```
  'readableDate',
  t => new Date(t * 1000).toGMTString()
);


const sanitizeMessage = getSet(
  'message',
  'message',
  msg => msg.replace(/</g, '&lt;')
);


const buildLinkToSender = getSet(
  'username',
  'sender',
  u => `https://example.com/users/${u}`
);


const srcLnk = ({sourceType, sourceId}) =>
  `https://example.com/${sourceType}/${sourceId}`;
const buildLinkToSource = (notification) => ({
  ...notification,
  source: srcLnk(notification),
});


const srcIcn = type =>
  `https://example.com/assets/icons/${type}-small.svg`;
const addIcon = getSet(
  'sourceType',
  'icon',
  srcIcn
);
```

Notice that each function is small. Most of them are but 3–5 lines. Some people find this distasteful. But, no single function is doing anything complex, except for processNotifications(). And even it does nothing but compose a total of six functions, making it eight lines long. It's almost trivial to inspect any specific function and work out what's going on.

Contrast our pipeline code to an imperative for-loop doing the same thing.

```
const imperativeProcessNotifications = (notifications) => {
  const base = 'https://example.com/'
  for (let notification of notifications) {
    let {sourceType, sourceId, username} = notification;
    notification.readableDate =
      new Date(notification.date * 1000).toGMTString();
    notification.message =
      notification.message.replace(/</g, '&lt;');
    notification.sender =
      `${base}users/${username}`;
    notification.source =
      `${base}${sourceType}/${sourceId}`;
    notification.icon =
      `${base}assets/icons/${sourceType}-small.svg`;
  }
  return notifications;
}
```

Some people prefer this because you can see everything happening all at once. And it's explicit about what the computer will be doing every step of the way. If we're familiar with for-loops, we can infer that it's doing some array processing. But we can't infer much more than that without reading each line. That may not be so bad with a small loop like this. But the more processing we add, the more difficult it becomes.

We can't argue that one version is simpler than the other. They're doing the same task. All that changes is where we describe the details. Neither can we argue that one version is more readable than the other; since that depends on what you're familiar with. We *can* argue though, that the `flow()` pipeline version is more *expressive*. It uses higher-level abstractions to communicate intent.

Often, you'll hear functional programmers enthuse that functional programming helps them *reason* about their code. This is the flip side of expressivity. We've expressed our code as relationships between pure functions. And because pure functions obey mathematical laws, we can make inferences and observe patterns. This in turn allows us to make performance optimisations or simplify the code. And we can do so with confidence we're not breaking anything.

§ 3.5. GREAT, TELL THAT TO MY TEAM FULL OF HATERS

It's one thing to know that functional programming lets you write more expressive code. It's another to get the rest of the team on board. Learning functional programming can be laborious if you're used to imperative code. Hence, it can be a hard sell when people are fine with the way they write code now. And it's even harder when there's bad history. Like when an enthusiastic junior writes a bunch of point-free code. Which then breaks. And so the senior dives in to try and fix it. But the style is so foreign that they can't work out what's going on. Even worse, they can't even insert a `console.log()` without breaking the code even more. The senior then ends up rewriting the whole thing from scratch and outlawing point-free style. And the team holds functional programming in suspicion from then on. Point-free? Pointless.

Now, I can't give you a magic argument that will convince anyone of the benefits of functional programming. I wish it were possible. But it doesn't work that way. We have to accept that programming is a social activity. Code is communication. Even on a solo project you're still communicating with your future self.

As Martin Fowler said:

> Any fool can write code that a computer can understand. Good programmers write code that humans can understand.[4]

Or, as Kent Beck put it:

> "Communicative" is not a property of the code but of the sociotechnical community that includes & maintains it.[5]

We have to write for our audience. If the team isn't ready for point-free functional pipelines, ramming it down their throats won't help.

We have some hope though. Good writing can educate as well as communicate. The same goes for code. Your audience will change over time. After all, the *You* who finishes reading this book won't be the same *You* who started it. If you introduce functional concepts bit-by-bit, over time, they will become familiar. And familiar becomes readable.

Remember too, that what's unreadable now, may not be in future. We all find new styles of content difficult to process. If I pick up a book of Shakespeare's plays, it's difficult for me to read because I'm not used to the old English. But that doesn't mean it's bad writing. And it doesn't mean I can't *learn* to read it. Similarly,

---

[4] Martin Fowler, Kent Beck, John Brant, William Opdyke, and Don Roberts, 1999, *Refactoring: Improving the Design of Existing Code*, Addison-Wesley, p. 15.
[5] Kent Beck, 2021, https://tinyurl.com/kent-beck-on-readability

when I first encountered Promises in JavaScript, I couldn't comprehend them. But smart people were enthusiastic about them. And they solved a real problem. So I learned to understand Promises. And they are much nicer than a callback pyramid of doom. It's the same with functional programming. Some techniques are hard to read and understand. But that doesn't mean that they're bad or useless. It means that they're not familiar *yet*. And the benefits are real.

Be prepared to defend any new concepts you introduce though. Make sure that they solve a real problem that *others agree is a problem*. And try not to get bogged down in debates about readability. They devolve into "Yes, it is," "No, it isn't," fast. Instead, try to steer the conversation towards expressivity and confidence. You're on much more solid ground then.

We'll talk more about expressivity and confidence in Chapter 7.

§ 3.6. BUT, MY TEAM STILL HAS TO READ MY CODE

Even if we end up having wonderful, polite conversations about expressivity, we still have a problem. If we're working programmers, we still need to write code. That's what we get paid for (more or less). Thus, we're caught in a dilemma:

- We want to write expressive code that we're confident about. Which implies writing in a functional style.
- But, we also want to write code that our team can comprehend and maintain. And that implies writing code that's *familiar* to the rest of the team.

It feels like we're forced to choose between writing good code and writing 'readable' code. But, when it comes to code style, these issues aren't always black and white.

It's important to understand that 'functional' isn't a binary property. We don't even have an official definition of 'functional programming'. This means that we can adjust how 'functional' our code *appears* to suit our audience. All we need to do is keep in mind one rule:

We prefer to work with pure functions (and expressions).

That's it. With this rule in mind, we can adjust almost any piece of code to *appear* more or less functional, without losing our confidence.

To give an example, let's look at our `processComments()` function from earlier:

```
const processNotifications = flow(
  map(readableDate),
  map(sanitizeMessage),
  map(buildLinkToSender),
  map(buildLinkToSource),
  map(addIcon),
  reduce((_, val) => val, fallback)
);
```

This kind of code might make some people nervous. There's lots of composition and currying going on. And higher-order functions all over the place. But what if we were to rewrite it using method calls?

```
const processNotifications = (rawNotifications) =>
  rawNotifications
    .map(readableDate)
    .map(sanitizeMessage)
    .map(buildLinkToSender)
```

```
.map(buildLinkToSource)
.map(addIcon)
.reduce((_, val) => val, fallback);
```

Lots of JavaScript developers are familiar with array methods. And programmers with an OOP background seem to *love* chained method calls. This small change may be enough for the rest of the team to figure out what's going on.

Now, we have lost a little flexibility here. This is because flow() has a bit more power than chained method calls. It will let us keep adding functions to the pipeline, even when there are no methods left to call. But for this particular case, we might not need that flexibility, so it's fine. We're still working with pure functions. And we're still composing simple, easy-to-understand functions together. We're just using a different approach.

In some cases though, this might not be enough. The team might still consider this code 'too clever'. Passing around functions without comforting fat arrows, might still be too much. Not a problem. We can adjust our code to add those warm, fuzzy fat arrows.

```
const processNotifications = (rawNotifications) =>
  rawNotifications
    .map(n => readableDate(n))
    .map(n => sanitizeMessage(n))
    .map(n => buildLinkToSender(n))
    .map(n => buildLinkToSource(n))
    .map(n => addIcon(n))
    .reduce((_, val) => val, fallback);
```

With this change, it's clear that the parameters we're passing to .map() are all functions. We *have* added an extra layer of function wrappers. And technically, that will be less efficient. For most cases though, it's unlikely to be an issue in modern browsers.[6]

It's still possible that this code is too clever by your team's standards though. Perhaps all this method chaining is still too much. In that case, we could create interstitial variables, to clarify what's going on:

```
const processNotifications = (rawNotifications) => {
  const withDate = rawNotifications
    .map(n => readableDate(n));
  const sanitized = withDate
    .map(n => sanitizeMessage(n));
  const withSender = sanitized
    .map(n => buildLinkToSender(n));
  const withSource = withSender
    .map(n => buildLinkToSource(n));
  const withIcon = withSource
    .map(n => addIcon(n));
  const notifications = withIcon
    .reduce((_, val) => val, fallback);
  return notifications;
};
```

We've now broken everything down into seven statements, each of which assigns a local variable. For some people, seeing that variable name gives them a little bit more context on what's happening to the data. And that helps them figure out what's going on with the code. And that's fine. If it helps our team read the code, we can add some variable names. Our code is still 'functional,' in that

---

[6] It's also possible that the JavaScript runtime might be clever enough to factor it out. And yes, for some applications, it might be a big deal. As with anything related to JavaScript performance, you'd need to measure to see if it makes a difference for your particular application.

we're still working with pure functions. We're still working with algebraic structures too. But we've made the code more verbose to aid the reader.

If this last version is so much more readable, though, why not write it this way in the first place? Why bother with fancy stuff like `flow()` and whatnot?

Well, as always, we're making trade offs here. In the last version, we've made the code noisier. That is, we've spelled things out to the point of redundancy. Each variable name repeats information already there in the call to `map()`. That might still be the right thing to do, depending on the team. But it's not without drawbacks.

All four versions of `processNotifications()` do the same thing. But each one emphasises different aspects of the code. All four versions are composing `map()` and `reduce()` operations. Some versions emphasise the *composition* part of it. Others emphasise what's happening at each step. As we discussed in Section 3.4, the `flow()` version of this code expresses a lot of information. That information is still there in the variable assignment version. But it may be buried under a lot of other information. The signal-to-noise ratio is different.

The point isn't to declare any of these four versions 'better' than the others. Rather, the point is to show that we can adjust our style to suit the needs of our team. The code is still 'functional' in each version. That is, we're working with referentially transparent functions. Hence we're free to adjust our style, without harming our confidence in the code.

FUNCTIONAL PROGRAMMING HARMS PERFORMANCE: RECURSION

Performance is a tricky subject. Not because the technical concepts are difficult to understand. (Though, sometimes they may be.) No, it's tricky because the situation is always changing. Hardware vendors release new devices each year. And browser vendors strive to outdo each other, releasing new builds each night. New APIs and optimisations make old approaches redundant. Not to mention just-in-time (JIT) compilers throwing in their surprises. As a result, it's hard to say anything definitive about JavaScript performance.

Worse still, every project is different. In one project, 0.1 ms delay may be the difference between success and failure. In another scenario, 100ms may not make a shred of difference. Some applications need to support browsers all the way back to IE9. Others need to run on low-power devices where every CPU instruction counts. Still other applications run on high-powered servers, rack-mounted in a data-centre right next to hydroelectric power stations. Some projects handle enormous amounts of data. Others display intricate moving graphics. Each situation has different nuances and complications.

To make this concrete, consider the humble array .map() method. It's possible to write a function that does the same thing:

```
const arrayMap = (f, arr) => {
  let ret = [];
  for (el of arr) {
    ret.push(f(el));
  }
  return ret;
}
```

For years, we *knew* that this for-loop version was always faster than the built-in array method. But that's no longer 100% true. Yes, the for-loop version is still faster in Chrome, Chrome's cousins,[1] and Firefox. But not in Safari. In Safari, the array method is faster. By a lot.

Whenever someone makes sweeping statements about performance in JavaScript, it pays to be skeptical. If it's a blog post or comment, check *when* it was written. Make sure to consider what kind of application they have in mind. Otherwise you may find yourself chasing the Ghost of Performance Past.

Now, none of this is to say that performance doesn't matter. It

---

[1] By this, I mean Chromium-based browsers like Microsoft Edge, Brave, Opera, and Vivaldi.

does. Nor are we saying that we can't have an intelligent conversation about performance. We can. But it's important to be clear what we're talking about. And taking real measurements trumps hypothetical suppositions.

The sad reality is that code written in a functional style *will* sometimes be slower than 'equivalent' imperative code. In JavaScript, at least. But, at the same time, we can also find cases where functional style happens to make the code much faster. In these two chapters we'll look at some hot spots that cause people trouble most often. These include recursion (this chapter) and immutable data (next chapter).

§ 4.1. RECURSION

A moment ago, we looked at an imperative implementation of array .map() using a for-loop. But functional programming doesn't have loops. Haskell, for example, has no language constructs like while or for. They don't exist. How then, does one write something like .map() without loops?

We use recursion.

Plain recursion is a technique where a function calls itself from inside its own definition. It may be confusing at first. But once you get used to it, recursion can be beautiful. Here's how we would use recursion to write arrayMap():

```
const recursiveArrayMap = f => arr => {
  if (arr.length === 0) return arr;
  const [x, ...rest] = arr;
  return [f(x), ...recursiveArrayMap(f)(rest)];
}
```

Notice that the first thing we do is check if it's time to stop recursing. In this case, by checking if the array is empty. Every recursive function needs some kind of test like this. It's a lot like the test condition in a while loop. If we don't have it, the recursion will continue forever. And at some point, our program will crash.

Notice also that `recursiveArrrayMap()` calls itself. You can spot it in the final return statement. This is what makes the function recursive.

Now, while this is a nice, neat little example, it doesn't solve a true problem. We already have other ways of doing `.map()`. There's little chance we'd ever use `recursiveArrayMap()` in the 'real world.' So let's try something a little more interesting. Recursive functions tend to work well with recursive data structures, like trees. And there's a tree structure that JavaScript developers work with all the time: The Document Object Model (DOM).

Let's see if we can create a function that will return a list of all elements below the `<main>` element. But we want to filter this list to elements that contain a text node. This includes elements like `<strong>` or `<em>` inside a paragraph. It also includes paragraphs (`<p>`) too.

Why would we ever want to do this? Well, we may want to do something like this if we're working on internationalisation or localization for an application. Most of the time, we can use `document.querySelectorAll()` to query the DOM tree. But CSS selectors aren't helpful for pulling out text nodes, so `.querySelectorAll()` can't help us.

Here's one way to write our utility function:

```
const hasTextChild = root => [...root.childNodes].some(
  el => el.nodeName === '#text'
);
```

```
const elsWithTextNode = (root) => {
  const retHead = hasTextChild(root) ? [root] : [];
  return retHead.concat(
    [...root.children].flatMap(
      (el) => elsWithTextNode(el)
    )
  );
};
```

This function will recurse through the tree, look for elements with text node children, and return them in document order.[2]

Now, whenever we look at a recursive function, it's important to identify the stopping condition. It has to be there, otherwise the function will keep running on forever. Hence, we should ask, where's the stopping condition for elsWithTextNode()? It's a little hard to see for this function, but it's there. It's in the spread [...root.children]. If we come across an array with no children, then our .flatMap() function will never call elsWithTextNodes(). And the recursion will stop.

There's a problem with both recursiveArrayMap() and elsWith-TextNode() though. They're limited. In most JavaScript engines, using recursiveArrayMap() on an array with more than 1000 elements will throw an error: Maximum call stack size exceeded. For example.

---

[2] You may have noticed that it would be easy to turn this into a more generic function. Instead of passing the single root parameter, we pass a predicate as well. We'd then have a function that would scan a DOM element tree and match all elements against the predicate. This would be neat, but .querySelectorAll() does a fine job of covering most use cases where we'd want that function. And .querySelectorAll() is almost always going to be much faster.

```
const bigArray = (new Array(2000))
  .fill().map((_, i) => i);
const itemise = x => '<li>${x}</li>';
const wontfinish = recursiveArrayMap(itemise)(bigArray);
// Maximum call stack size exceeded
```

What's going on behind the scenes is that the interpreter[3] uses a data structure called a stack to keep track of function calls. Every time we call a function, the interpreter allocates space on the stack to keep track of where to go back when the function returns. Then, once the function finishes execution, the interpreter 'pops' that data off the call stack and frees up memory. When we call another function, the interpreter 'pushes' another entry onto the stack, which takes up memory.

To keep memory usage from getting out of hand, JavaScript interpreters limit the size of the stack. And the limit is rather small. At least, small compared to the size of arrays we may want to map over. That makes recursiveArrayMap() impractical as well as slow.

PROPER TAIL CALLS

There's a section of the ECMAScript standard[4] that *ought* to help here. It's called Proper Tail Calls (PTC). It's a standard relating to recursive functions. In particular, it relates to the case of a func-

---

[3] To be accurate, we can't call JavaScript runtime engines 'interpreters' any more. They don't strictly run through our script, line-by-line and execute each statement in order. Modern JavaScript runtimes run all kinds of fancy optimisation tricks like JIT compilation to make everything run fast. For simplicity though, I'll keep referring to the 'JavaScript runtime engine' as an 'interpreter' throughout the book. Mainly because it gets tedious to write 'JavaScript runtie engine' over and over again. And it's tedious to read, too.

[4] The *ECMAScript standard* (https://tc39.es/ecma262/) is the formal name for the document that specifies the JavaScript language. There's a whole story to why it's called the *ECMAScript standard* and not the JavaScript standard. And also why it's associated with something called TC39. Getting into the details is a bit beyond the scope of this book though.

tion where the last thing it does is call another function and return the reuslt. We refer to this last function invocation as a *tail call.*

The specification states that, in that specific case, there's no point in holding on to the stack entry. And it mandates that browsers must throw that entry away. What does this mean in practice? If we move our recursive call to the tail call position, then we will never blow the stack limit. We can recurse as much as we want.

If we're to take advantage of this, we need to do some work. Our example functions recursiveArrayMap() and elsWithTextNode() don't have the recursive bit in tail call position. We need to change them. In both examples, we'll create a helper function. Then we use the helper function to make the recursive call the last thing the function does.

First, recursiveArrayMap():

```
const recursiveArrayMap = f => arr => {
  // We'll call our helper function 'go'
  const go = (processed , toProcess) => {
    if (toProcess.length == 0) return processed;
    const [a, ...rest] = toProcess;
    const newProcessed = [...processed, f(a)];
    return go(newProcessed, rest);
  }
  return go([], arr);
}
```

The helper function go(), looks much like our earlier version of recursiveArrayMap(). The main difference is that it takes a second argument, processed. This allows us to do the concatenation (creating newProcessed) before we make the recursive call. And that moves the recursive call to go() into the tail call position.

We can do something much the same for `elsWithTextNode()`.

```
const hasTextChild = root => Array.prototype.some.call(
  root.childNodes,
  el => el.nodeName === '#text'
);


const elsWithTextNode = root => {
  const go = (processed, toProcess) => {
    if (toProcess.length == 0) return processed;
    const [el, ...rest] = toProcess;
    const newProcessed = (hasTextChild(el))
      ? [...processed, el]
      : processed;
    return go(newProcessed, [...rest, ...el.children]);
  }
  return go([], [root]);
}
```

With these new tail call versions, if you run them in Safari, that stack limit error goes away. On both Mac and iOS. But, alas, in other browsers (at the time of writing), the issue remains. The Chrome V8 team did add PTC at one point. Then later, they stripped it out again, declaring it provided a confusing debugging experience. Hence, the situation won't change soon, unless something radical happens with the V8 team.

With that, it's understandable if you're thinking all these tail call shenanigans are a waste of time. After all, if it's never going to get wide browser support, why bother? But this tail call technique opens up *another* technique we can use to speed up recursive functions.

Trampolining lets us do what the interpreter would do with PTC, by hand. That is, when the interpreter does PTC optimisation, it doesn't keep track of every call to our recursive function. Instead, it keeps track of only the most recent call. And when the recursion terminates, it returns the final value. With trampolining, we write a helper function that manages this for us.

To make our trampoline function work though, we need to adjust the two go() functions. We change them so that they return a 'thunk' instead of running the calculation straight away.

If you've not come across thunks before, they may sound a little scary. But it's a fancy name for something straightforward. The term means 'delayed calculation.' We can turn any JavaScript expression into a thunk by sticking () => in front of it. By turning the expression into a function, we delay the calculation until the function is called.

Adjusting the go() function inside recursiveArrayMap() looks like so:

```javascript
const go = (processed, toProcess) => {
  if (toProcess.length == 0) return processed;
  const [a, ...rest] = toProcess;
  const newProcessed = [...processed, f(a)];
  // We return a thunk on the next line instead of
  // calling go()
  return () => go(newProcessed, rest);
}
```

It's not much different from the earlier version. The main change is that now, we return a thunk instead of the final value.

The change for go() inside elsWithTextNode() is not much different:

```
const go = (processed, toProcess) => {
  if (toProcess.length == 0) return processed;
  const [el, ...rest] = toProcess;
  const newProcessed = (hasTextChild(el))
    ? [...processed, el]
    : processed;
  // Return a thunk instead of calling go()
  return () => go(
    newProcessed,
    [...rest, ...el.children]
  );
}
```

Both recursive helpers now return thunks. As soon as we call go(), it returns a function, and execution stops. We need something to help it jump back into action. That's where the trampoline comes in. It runs our thunks in a loop, without recursion, and returns the final result. It looks like so:

```
const trampoline = (f, ...args) => {
  let next = f.apply(f, args);
  while (typeof next == 'function') {
    next = next();
  }
  return next;
}
```

It's not super complicated. It takes a function (optionally with arguments) and runs it. When it stops, it checks to see if we have a function. If so, we assume it's a thunk and bounce on. At some point though, we will get a value and return.[5]

---

[5] And, yes, it's a problem if we want our recursive function to return a function

Adding that to our `recursiveArrayMap()` function looks like this:

```
const recursiveArrayMap = f => arr => {
  const go = (processed, toProcess) => {
    if (toProcess.length == 0) return processed;
    const [a, ...rest] = toProcess;
    const newProcessed = [...processed, f(a)];
    return () => go(newProcessed, rest);
  }
  return trampoline(go, [], arr);
}
```

And here's how `trampoline()` works with `elsWithTextNodes()`:

```
const elsWithTextNode = (root) => {
  const go = (processed, toProcess) => {
    if (toProcess.length == 0) return processed;
    const [el, ...rest] = toProcess;
    const newProcessed = (hasTextChild(el))
      ? [...processed, el]
      : processed;
    return () => go(
      newProcessed,
      [...rest, ...el.children]
    );
  };
  return trampoline(go, [], [root]);
}
```

With that in place, we no longer hit the stack limit.

---

as its final result.

Now, after all that, let's take one final look at that trampoline function:

```
const trampoline = (f, ...args) => {
  let next = f.apply(f, args);
  while (typeof next == 'function') {
    next = next();
  }
  return next;
}
```

Someone may still be thinking "That trampoline function doesn't look too functional." And that's true. It's got a while-loop, and we're mutating a local variable. The code is all rather... imperative.

Let's think about what we're doing here though. We're taking a recursive function and manually performing the same kind of tail call elimination that the JavaScript interpreter might apply. It needs to use imperative code because otherwise we'd end up trying to optimise recursion using more recursion. Even though it's made with some imperative code we usually try to avoid, trampoline() is a little magical. It makes the impossible, possible.

§ 4.2. MEASURE

We discussed earlier that it's hard to say anything definitive about JavaScript performance without measuring. And these recursive functions are a classic case study. Suppose we were to measure the performance of our recursiveArrayMap() functions. We could create ten arrays with varying lengths. Then run a simple operation on each array and measure how long it takes. And we'd want to do that a few times, to get a statistical sample.

I ran these measurements using a tool called JSBench,[6] and the results were interesting. You can see the charts in figs. 4.1 to 4.3. And I've recorded the actual numbers for each chart in Appendix E.

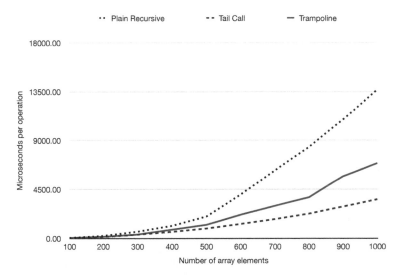

Figure 4.1: **Chrome 104.0.** Time taken to run a recursive array map operation. Lower is better. MacBook Pro (16-inch, 2019), 2.6 GHz 6-Core Intel Core i7.

We can see some interesting things in these charts. For Chrome, the numbers are as we'd expect. The tail call version is the fastest. And it's not so different from the trampoline version, which incurs a little overhead from extra function calls. The plain recursive version is slowest, and it gets slower and slower with more array elements.

Looking at Firefox, though, the lines are more interesting. The plain recursive function starts off slowest. But the tail call and trampoline versions get slower with more array elements. And for

---

[6] You can find the code I used to generate the array and run the tests at https://jsbench.me/wel7cvlrs0.

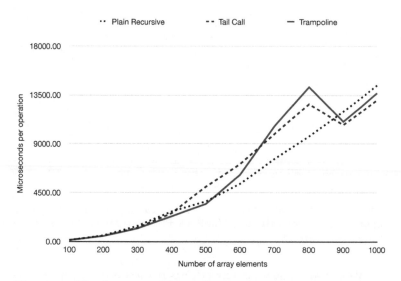

Figure 4.2: **Firefox 104.0.** Time taken to run a recursive array map operation. Lower is better. MacBook Pro (16-inch, 2019), 2.6 GHz 6-Core Intel Core i7.

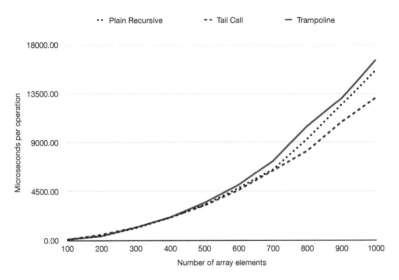

Figure 4.3: **Safari 15.6.1.** Time taken to run a recursive array map operation. Lower is better. MacBook Pro (16-inch, 2019), 2.6 GHz 6-Core Intel Core i7.

a while, the plain recursive function becomes the fastest. Then, somewhere around 800–900 elements, Firefox changes something, and the plain recursive version is slowest again.

With Safari, there's not much difference between all three functions. The plain recursive version is slower than the tail-call, but faster than the trampoline.

Notice how in all three browsers, the lines curve upward. This suggests that there's something going on besides the recursion. And indeed, we're doing a lot of copying values into new arrays. We might hypothesise that this is the source of the exponential slowdown. And we can test this by replacing the plain JavaScript arrays with immutable data structures from the Immutable[7] library. (We'll talk more about immutable data next chapter). The plain recursive version might look like so:

```
const {Stack} = Immutable;

const recursiveArrayMap = f => arr => {
  const go = stack => {
    if (stack.size === 0) return stack;
    const x = stack.first();
    return go(stack.pop()).push(f(x));
  }
  return go(Stack(arr)).toArray();
}
```

While the tail-call version becomes:

```
const {List, Stack} = Immutable;
```

---

[7] You can read more about Immutable at: https://immutable-js.com

```
const recursiveArrayMap = f => arr => {
  const go = (processed, toProcess) => {
    if (toProcess.size === 0) return processed;
    const x = toProcess.first()
    return go(processed.push(f(x)), toProcess.shift());
  };
  return go(List(), Stack(arr)).toArray();
};
```

And the trampoline version is similar:

```
const {List, Stack} = Immutable;

const recursiveArrayMap = f => arr => {
  const go = (processed, toProcess) => {
    if (toProcess.size === 0) return processed;
    const x = toProcess.first()
    return () => go(processed.push(f(x)), toProcess.shift());
  };
  return trampoline(go, List(), Stack(arr)).toArray();
};
```

Running the experiment again, we get a new set of charts, as shown in figs. 4.4 to 4.6

With Immutable in place, then performance improves across the board. The run time increases linearly with the length of the array. And notice that the simple recursive option is now the fastest, across all three browsers. This is likely because it makes effective use of Stack, which is an efficient data structure if all we need is .first() and .shift().

But what about our DOM traversal example? How does that perform? To test that, we run a similar experiment. But, instead of

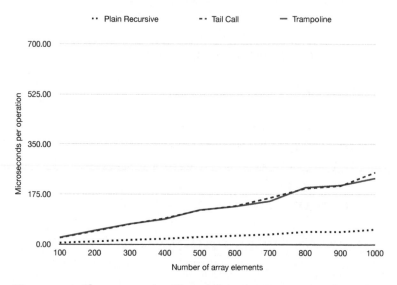

Figure 4.4: **Chrome 104.0.** Time taken to run a recursive array map operation using immutable data structures. Lower is better. MacBook Pro (16-inch, 2019), 2.6 GHz 6-Core Intel Core i7.

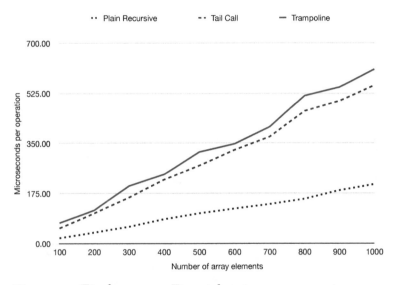

Figure 4.5: **Firefox 104.0.** Time taken to run a recursive array map operation using immutable data structures. Lower is better. MacBook Pro (16-inch, 2019), 2.6 GHz 6-Core Intel Core i7.

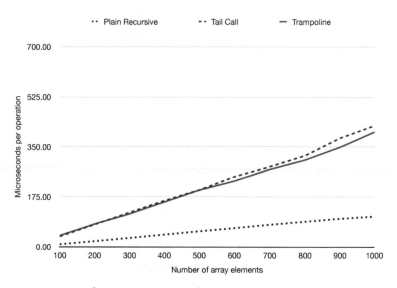

Figure 4.6: **Safari 15.6.1.** Time taken to run a recursive array map operation using immutable data structures. Lower is better. MacBook Pro (16-inch, 2019), 2.6 GHz 6-Core Intel Core i7.

creating an array and varying its length, we create a DOM tree and vary its depth.[8] Doing that, we get the charts shown in figs. 4.7 to 4.9

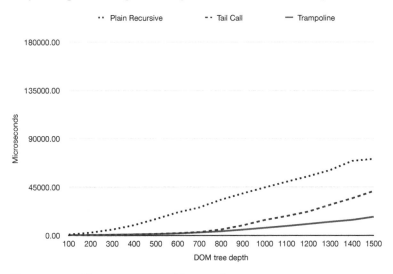

Figure 4.7: **Chrome 105.0.** Time taken to run a recursive DOM traversal. Lower is better. MacBook Pro (16-inch, 2019), 2.6 GHz 6-Core Intel Core i7.

Looking at these charts, once again, Chrome behaves much as we'd expect. The plain recursive approach is the slowest. And as we increase depth, the trampoline approach performs better than plain tail call. The slope of the curves is shallow, but still trending upward. In Firefox though, everything changes. The plain recursive approach starts out slower, but, as we increase DOM depth, it proves much faster than the other two approaches. And the tail call and trampoline approaches both increase exponentially. With Safari, though, the results are bumpy. The tail call and trampoline approaches show much the same performance. But both are slower than the plain recursive approach.

---

[8] You can find the code I used to generate the DOM tree and run the tests at https://jsbench.me/t0l7csa04i.

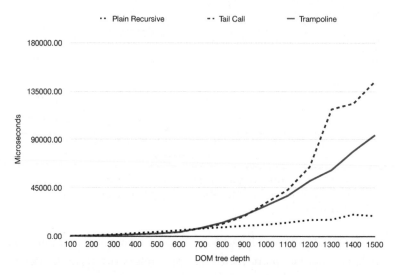

Figure 4.8: **Firefox 104.0.** Time taken to run a recursive DOM traversal. Lower is better. MacBook Pro (16-inch, 2019), 2.6 GHz 6-Core Intel Core i7.

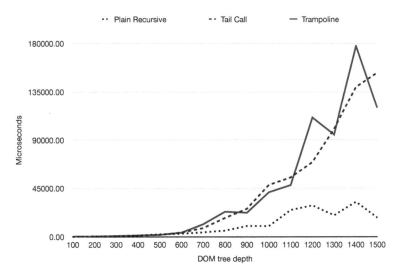

Figure 4.9: **Safari 15.6.1.** Time taken to run a recursive DOM traversal. Lower is better. MacBook Pro (16-inch, 2019), 2.6 GHz 6-Core Intel Core i7.

Now, with the recursive array map example, we saw a large improvement when we used immutable data structures. Will we see the same kind of improvement if we do something similar for DOM traversal? Let's try it and find out. Our plain recursive DOM traversal function looks like so:

```
const {Stack, List} = Immutable;

const elsWithTextNode = (root) => {
  const go = (el) => {
    const childrenWithTextNodes = Stack(el.children ?? [])
      .flatMap(go);
    return hasTextChild(el)
      ? childrenWithTextNodes.unshift(el)
      : childrenWithTextNodes;
  };
  return go(root).toArray();
};
```

The tail call version becomes:

```
const elsWithTextNode = root => {
  const go = (processed, toProcess) => {
    if (toProcess.size == 0) return processed;
    const el = toProcess.first();
    const rest = toProcess.shift();
    const newProcessed = (hasTextChild(el))
      ? processed.push(el)
      : processed;
    return () => go(
      newProcessed,
```

```
    List(el.children).concat(rest)
    );
  }
  return trampoline(go(List(), List.of(root))).toArray();
};
```

And the trampoline version is similar:

```
const elsWithTextNode = (root) => {
  const go = (processed, toProcess) => {
    if (toProcess.size == 0) return processed;
    const el = toProcess.first();
    const rest = toProcess.shift();
    const newProcessed = (hasTextChild(el))
      ? processed.push(el)
      : processed;
    return go(
      newProcessed,
      List(el.children).concat(rest)
    );
  }
  return go(List(), List.of(root)).toArray();
};
```

If we run our performance comparison against those, we get
the results shown in figs. 4.10 to 4.12.

Looking at these results, we see that this time, immutable data
structures make the tail call and trampoline versions much faster.
And this is consistent across all three browsers. The story with
the plain recursive version is rather sorry though. In Chrome, it
hits some kind of recursion limit and can't handle any more than
a depth of 300. And this is odd, since 300 is a lot less than the stack

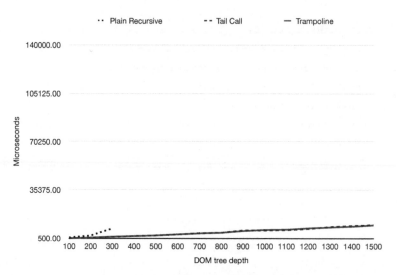

Figure 4.10: **Chrome 105.0.** Time taken to run a recursive DOM traversal using immutable data structures. Lower is better. Mac-Book Pro (16-inch, 2019), 2.6 GHz 6-Core Intel Core i7.

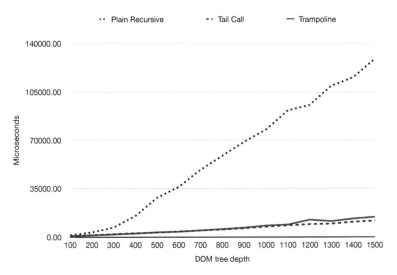

Figure 4.11: **Firefox 104.0.** Time taken to run a recursive DOM traversal using immutable data structures. Lower is better. MacBook Pro (16-inch, 2019), 2.6 GHz 6-Core Intel Core i7.

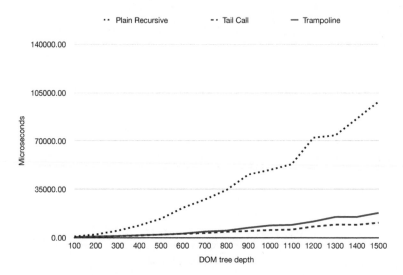

Figure 4.12: **Safari 15.6.1.** Time taken to run a recursive DOM traversal using immutable data structures. Lower is better. MacBook Pro (16-inch, 2019), 2.6 GHz 6-Core Intel Core i7.

size limit. Which implies that the Stack data structure from Immutable is doing some recursion of its own. But we don't see Firefox or Safari hitting a stack limit. Which is even more odd. Still, in both Firefox and Safari, the plain recursive version is slower than the other two. And from this we can infer that perhaps Stack's `.flatMap()` method isn't well optimised compared to List's `.concat()` method.

What can we learn from all this, though? The short answer is that it's imporatant to measure performance. And the choice of data structure has a larger impact on performance than whether we use recursion or not. Recursion is a tool. A powerful tool. Sure, it can be dangerous. But so can loops. We want to learn to use our tools with wisdom and discretion.

§ 4.3. PERFORMANCE AND REFERENTIAL TRANSPARENCY

Imperative loops will often be faster than recursion in JavaScript. Even with our fancy trampoline, the imperative version of `arrayMap()` is faster than the recursive one. JavaScript interpreters aren't optimised for this style of code.

What do we do then? Do we give up and go back to for-loops with our tail between our legs? I say no. Because functional programming itself tells us that using the imperative version of `arrayMap()` is fine.[9]

How is that? Well, in functional programming we like to work with pure functions as much as possible. And we do this because pure functions have this property of referential transparency.

To clarify what we mean here:

1. Pure functions are functions that always return the same output, given the same input, without causing side effects.

---

[9] Though, using the built-in array methods may be even better.

2. Referential transparency is a property where I can take the result of a calculation and substitute it anywhere I had the calculation itself. If the calculation was referentially transparent, I'm guaranteed to get the same result.

To make this concrete, suppose we take our `itemise()` function from earlier. If I call `itemise()` with the string `"Moriarty"`, I get back another string: `"<li>Moriarty</li>"`. Now, referential transparency means that anywhere I see the code `itemise("Moriarty")` I can replace that with `"<li>Moriarty</li>"`, and be guaranteed that the result will not change.

Taking those two properties of referential transparency together, we can draw an inference. Suppose we can show that our imperative `arrayMap()` always produces the same results as `recursiveArrayMap()`. That is, `arrayMap()` is a referentially transparent, pure function. Then we know, with certainty, we can substitute one for the other without changing our program's behaviour. In other words, we can switch to the faster version of `arrayMap()` without worrying that our code will break. And without changing anything *other than* the mapping function.

To recap, yes, recursion is slow and limited in JavaScript. We reach the call stack limit with modest sized arrays. And JavaScript interpreters don't optimize for slinging functions around like that. But, as we've seen, we can find ways around this. And even though recursion can sometimes be slow, it's exceptionally useful as a problem-solving tool. Even if we end up rewriting all our recursive functions with imperative loops, *thinking* recursively is incredibly useful. Recursive functions and data structures allow us to break complex problems into manageable chunks. Sure, we may have to rewrite our code in a more performant way. But recursive thinking gives us access to elegant solutions.

There's more than one reason why people complain functional

programming harms performance, though. In the next chapter we'll look at immutable data.

FUNCTIONAL PROGRAMMING HARMS PERFORMANCE: IMMUTABLE DATA

Another reason people complain about functional performance is when inexperienced developers get a little over-zealous about avoiding mutation. Somewhere along the way, they learn that functional programmers never mutate any program state. ('Program state' is a fancy way of referring to data in memory.) And, as a result, they end up writing inefficient code.

The most common example is recreating an object over-and-over again in a reducer function. For example, imagine we need a utility function. One that takes an array of objects, and converts it to a single object, where the keys come from some field in each array item. We may write something like this:

```
// This is a bad example, don't copy it.
const keyBy = (key, arr) => arr.reduce(
  (acc, item) => ({...acc, [item[key]]: item,}),
  {}
);
```

This utility function works by folding (reducing) over each item in the array. For each new item, we grab the key name, and return a new object with all the accumulated values. That is, all the values so far, *plus* the new key-item pair.

If the input array is small, this isn't a big deal. But we end up copying a lot of values. Because each time we add an item, we copy all the other items we've copied before, too. To be precise, the number of values copied is given by the triangular number sequence:

$$T_n = \sum_{k=1}^{n} k = \frac{n(n+1)}{2}$$

Where n is the number of key-value pairs in the object, and T_n is the total number of values copied. For 10 values, we end up making 55 copies. For 20 values, it's 210 copies. For 100 values, we get 5,050 copies! That cost adds up fast. It's inefficient code.

We can see similar problems in `recursiveArrayMap()` and `elsWithTextNode()` from last chapter, too.

Why do people do this? Somewhere along the way, they've picked up the idea that mutating data is bad. And the question is, why? What's so wrong with mutating data?

The short answer is that there's nothing wrong with mutating data. Mutable state is fine. It's *shared* mutable state that's the problem.

That's worth repeating:

- Shared state is fine, so long as we don't mutate it.
- Mutating state is fine, so long as we don't share it.

We can fix our keyBy() example by introducing a small amount of mutation.

```
const keyBy = (key, arr) => {
  const init = {};
  const keyByReducer = (acc, item) => {
    acc[item[key]] = item;
    return acc;
  };
  return arr.reduce(keyByReducer, init);
};
```

There's now mutation going on. But we're not mutating any *shared* data. We don't change either of the arguments key or arr. And we don't reach outside the function scope to change any global variables either.

Wait a moment though. We mutate the init object. And then return it. Isn't that sharing mutable state?

It's not, because the function doesn't keep any reference to the return value. Once the function returns, it's gone. It can never touch that object again.

What about keyByReducer() though? It's modifying one of its arguments, every time it's called. How is that okay?

It would *not* be okay if we used keyByReducer() anywhere outside of keyBy(). But we don't. It exists solely within the scope of keyBy(). It doesn't reach outside of keyBy()'s scope. It modifies one variable, init, which ends up becoming our return value. And, as we discussed, once the function returns, it's gone. It's no longer shared.

In short, there's no sharing of mutated data outside the scope of `keyBy()`.

§ 5.1.   BUT, WHY?

If we're careful, we can manage mutations. We can write them in such a way that they don't leak outside a function scope. In practice, you'll find that most functional programmers tend to avoid mutation entirely. At least, until performance becomes an issue. Or, they'll use immutable data structures *designed* to offer improved performance. But, you may be wondering, why do they bother? Who cares if we mutate our data? Why is this even an issue?

The reason is, if we avoid mutation and side effects, we can treat functions *as if* they were mathematical functions. We call functions like this 'pure' functions. And, as we discussed earlier, pure functions are referentially transparent.

If we keep things pure, then we can ~~steal~~ borrow a whole bunch of mathematical reasoning and apply it to our code. We can apply laws to make safe automatic refactors (like we saw in Section 2.5 with the composition law). We can write performance optimisations with confidence that our code won't break.

If we start mutating shared state though, the deal is off. The mathematicians take their metaphorical ball and go home. No more laws. No more theorems. You're on your own playing the role of JavaScript interpreter in your head. But if we *can* assume no mutation of shared state (and no side effects), we get to work with pure functions. And pure functions give us confidence in our code. We can trust that if we put the same input in, we get the same value out.

Not everyone will find this argument convincing though. For example, imagine someone says: "I hate functional programming because it means dealing with immutable data all the time." It's not a great counter argument to say that immutable data is great because it lets us do functional programming. But we have other reasons for avoiding shared mutable state.

§ 5.2. IMMUTABLE DATA AND THE VIRTUAL DOM

It's a little ironic, but one of the most common reasons we avoid mutating shared state is to improve performance. Because assuming immutable data makes it possible to ask "Has something changed?"

Modern web frameworks, like React, are designed with the philosophy: Avoid unnecessary DOM operations. If we can help it, we'd like to avoid traversing the DOM. And avoid reading attributes from the DOM. And most of all, avoid changing the DOM. That is, unless it's absolutely necessary. To achieve this, a lot of modern JavaScript frameworks use a tool called the Virtual DOM.[1] A Virtual DOM is a tree of plain objects. The framework keeps each object as lightweight as possible. And each object holds information describing how the DOM ought to look.

When something changes the state of the application, the framework builds a new Virtual DOM tree. It then compares the new tree to the old one, to work out what's changed. Then, knowing what's changed, it builds a list of DOM operations to run. Running these operations makes the real DOM match the Virtual DOM.

The performance boost comes from never touching the DOM any more than necessary. Hence the goal is to keep that list of changes small. But, for that, we need to work out what's changed.

---

[1] A virtual DOM isn't the only way to avoid unnecessary DOM interactions. Svelte, for example, takes a different approach. It uses a build step to determine a minimal set of DOM interactions. But it can only do this by restricting the way you write code for components. Some people are happy to make that trade off. Others may have different preferences and needs.

Immutable data and the virtual DOM | 99

If we mutate a Virtual DOM object, it's impossible to tell what's changed. We no longer have access to the old state. Thus, we *must* use immutable data when working with a Virtual DOM.

React will even take this one step further. In React we can create components that are (conceptually) pure functions. They take Props and State and return a new React Element. React uses the returned Element to build the Virtual DOM. But, if we know that neither the Props nor the State have changed, then the output won't change either. In that case, there's no reason to re-run the Component code to get a new Element. We can use the old one, with no DOM update operations necessary.

Again, this works if:

1. We can tell if something has changed; and
2. Working out what's changed is faster than updating the DOM.

   It all hinges on immutable data.

§ 5.3. MEMOIZATION

The Virtual DOM isn't the only place where immutable data (and functional programming) can help improve performance. For example, we've already seen how we can use the Functor composition law to avoid creating intermediate arrays. We can find lots of other examples. One of the most common you'll come across in JavaScript is memoization.

(If you're already familiar with memoization, feel free to jump ahead to Section 5.4.)

Memoization is a technique for avoiding unnecessary calculations. But it only works if we can be sure of referential transparency. If there's side effects involved, then memoization will break your code.

Here's how we write a basic `memoize()` function:

```
const memoize = (func) => {
  const calculatedValues = new Map();
  return arg => {
    if (!calculatedValues.has(arg)) {
      calculatedValues.set(arg, func(arg));
    }
    return calculatedValues.get(arg);
  };
};
```

First, we create a new Map object in a closure. That is, we create a private variable that's visible to the function we return, but not outside it. This is our store for calculated values, so we call it calculatedValues.

Next, we return an anonymous function that takes a single argument, arg. When we call this function, it looks in calculatedValues to see if we've already calculated a value for this argument. If not, it runs the function, func(), and stores the result. After that, it returns the stored value. In short, it's like a cache for functions.

To illustrate how it works, let's imagine we're building a conference website. We're creating a schedule for the conference and have lots of academics presenting talks and workshops. Academics can be... *particular* about their names and titles. Hence, we'll write a function to make sure we format everyone's qualifications as expected.

Here's how the data might look:

```
const presenters = [
  {
    familyName: 'Potts'
    givenName: 'Bottomsly',
```

```
      preferredNameOrder: 'GIVEN_NAME_FIRST',
      honorific: 'Prof',
      qualifications: ['PhD', 'MSc', 'BSc'],
      institutions: ['Australian National University'],
    },
    // ... and so on
  ]
```

And here's a function for formatting an academic's name:[2]

```
const formatName = ({
    honorific,
    preferredNameOrder,
    givenName,
    familyName,
    qualifications,
  }) => [
    honorific ?? '',
    preferredNameOrder === 'GIVEN_NAME_FIRST'
      ? givenName
      : familyName,
    preferedNameOrder === 'GIVEN_NAME_FIRST',
      ? familyName
      : givenName,
    honorific == null
      ? academic.qualifications.join(', ')
      : '',
```

---

[2] Yes, I am well aware that names are much more complicated than presented in this function. If you'd like to learn more about this, check out *Falsehoods Programmers Believe About Names* by Patrick McKenzie: https://www.kalzumeus.com/2010/06/17/falsehoods-programmers-believe-about-names/.

```
].join('').trim();
```

We can create a memoized version of this function as follows:

```
const formatNameMemo = memoize(formatName);
```

Now, if we use `formatNameMemo()` instead of `formatname()`, we run that calculation once for any given academic.

Our `memoize()` function isn't magic though. There's limits to what it can improve. For example, it only works on unary functions. That is, functions that take a single argument. It doesn't work on functions that take more than one argument. We can work around it a little with currying. But trying to memoize a multivariate function is often a bit tricky.

It also falls down if we never call a memoized function with the same value more than once. For example, suppose we ran this code:

```
const presenterNames = presenters.map(formatNameMemo);
```

If we then went on to use `presenterNames`, and never called `formatNameMemo()` again. In that scenario, using `formatNameMemo()` makes the code *slower* than it needs to be. It takes more time to store results in the `Map` and look them up again. If we never need a particular calculation more than once, then memoizing will slow the code down.

We also face the problem that it's difficult to compare objects. For example, imagine we have two objects like so:

```
const professorX = {
    familyName: 'Xavier',
```

```
   givenName: 'Charles',
   honorific: 'Professor',
   preferredNameOrder: 'GIVEN_NAME_FIRST',
   qualifications: [],
   institutions: ['Xavier's school for gifted youngsters'],
};


const professorY = { ...professorX };
```

The values held in professorX and professorY are the same.
But, if we run the following, we get no performance improvement:

```
const xName = formatNameMemo(professorX);
const yName = formatNameMemo(professorY);
```

This is because professorX and professorY are two separate,
mutable variables. They don't share the actual values. The professorX variable is a reference to a location in memory where we
can look up its values. The professorY variable points to *another*
location in memory where we can look up *its* values. They're two
different references. When memoize() looks up professorY, it goes
through its entries to see if it's already done a calculation for that
memory location. And for professorY it hasn't, even though we've
already processed professorX.

How can we tell if professorX has the 'same' values as professorY? Well, we have to hand-code some kind of function that looks
at each key-value pair. Or, import one someone else has written.
JavaScript won't help us. Not even if we Object.freeze() our objects. They're still distinct references.

It's for this reason that the records and tuples TC39 proposal excites lots of JavaScript developers. At the time of writing, it's a stage 2 proposal.

> [The] proposal introduces two new deeply immutable data
> structures to JavaScript:
>
> * Record, a deeply immutable Object-like structure #{ x: 1, y:
>   2 }
> * Tuple, a deeply immutable Array-like structure #[1, 2, 3,
>   4]
>
> Records and Tuples can only contain primitives and other
> Records and Tuples.[3]

To put it another way, records & tuples will be truly immutable, not just frozen. When we compare them, equality "works like that of other JavaScript primitive types like Boolean and String values, comparing by contents, not identity."[4]

For example, with records and tuples, we could rewrite our professors like so:

```
const professorX = #{
  familyName: 'Xavier',
  givenName: 'Charles',
  honorific: 'Professor',
  preferredNameOrder: 'GIVEN_NAME_FIRST',
  qualifications: #[],
  institutions: #['Xavier's school for gifted youngsters'],
};
```

---

[3] ECMAScript proposal for the Record and Tuple value types:
https://github.com/tc39/proposal-record-tuple
[4] ECMAScript proposal for the Record and Tuple value types:
https://github.com/tc39/proposal-record-tuple

```
const professorY = #{ ...professorX };

professorX === professorY // true
```

With records and tuples, our memoization function could compare by *value* rather than *reference*.

Now, we can't get our hopes up too high. There's nothing in the proposal that guarantees comparing two large Records (or two large Tuples) will be a fast operation. But, even if that's the case, it will still make it more *convenient* to work with immutable data.

§ 5.5. WHAT DO WE DO IN THE MEANTIME?

At the time of writing, browsers haven't implemented the Records and Tuples proposal yet. For now, we're stuck with Babel transformations if we want to use them straight away. But we don't *have* to resort to Babel transformations. We have lots of immutable data libraries to choose from.

We do need to be careful though. Different 'immutable' libraries take different philosophical approaches. We can divide them into two categories:

1. Some help with the kind of task that the Records and Tuples proposal help with.
2. Others, try to make it difficult to mutate objects (and arrays) by accident.

PERSISTENT DATA STRUCTURES WITH STRUCTURAL SHARING

Libraries in the first category tend to use an approach called structural sharing. That is, they use clever data structures to provide data re-use. For example, consider adding a single item to an array. Without structural sharing, if we want to avoid mutation, we have to create a new array. And this would involve copying lots of values (as we saw last chapter). For example:

```
const baseArray = [0, 1, 2, 3];
const newArray = [...baseArray, 4];
```

That spread operator (...) *copies* all the values from baseArray into newArray. A structural sharing approach is different though. Instead of copying the entire list, we keep a reference to the base list. For example:

```
const baseList =
  { val: 3, next:
    { val: 2, next:
      { val: 1, next:
        { val: 0, next: undefined
}}}};
const newList = { val: 4, next: baseList };
```

This may look awkward on the surface. In practice though, structural sharing libraries have functions and methods that make working with them much more pleasant. Some more popular libraries in this category include:

- Immutable: https://immutable-js.com; and
- Mori: http://swannodette.github.io/mori/

IMMUTABLE HELPERS

The downside of the structural sharing libraries is that we lose some interoperability. That is, instead of using plain ol' JavaScript arrays, we use a class like List or Stack. We have to call methods like .get() to access values, instead of square brackets or property access. And this can be annoying. To address these frustrations, the other category of immutable libraries try to offer easy interoperability with plain JavaScript data. But they do this while helping prevent accidental mutation. Behind the scenes, they're often using something like Object.freeze().

Some helper libraries in this category include:

- Immer: https://immerjs.github.io/immer/;
- Seamless Immutable: https://github.com/rtfeldman/seamless-immutable; and
- Icepick: https://github.com/aearly/icepick.

The drawback of these approaches is that they will often still result in lots of copied values. And, as we saw, this can slow everything down a lot if you have a lot of data to handle.

§ 5.6. BUT, PERFORMANCE MATTERS

It's true. JavaScript isn't optimised for slinging immutable data around. Hence functional code will sometimes be a little slower than 'equivalent' code in an imperative style. But in practice, it's rare for this to be an issue. In most professional JavaScript work, performance bottlenecks aren't caused by over-use of functional techniques. We have myriad other, more significant, performance concerns to worry about. Like exploding bundle sizes, random 3rd party scripts interfering with load, and balancing Time to Interactive (TTI) with making necessary user data available.

That said, yes, we need to be careful. As we've seen, recursion can be a problem. And zealously avoiding mutation can also cause issues. But we've also seen how it's possible to work around these issues. It's important to remember that we don't use recursion and immutable data because they are blessed and holy. They're thinking tools. Two tools, out of lots in the functional tool box. We use them to solve problems, not to achieve some kind of moral superiority. They help us break a problem down into small, easy-to-handle chunks. And functional programming gives us other tools to compose a solution from all the smaller solutions for each chunk.

These tools are brilliant enough on their own. But again, as we've seen, referential transparency *also* helps us optimise our solutions. We can take one part of the solution and replace it with a faster version. We can apply techniques like memoization. And we can make these changes with confidence. Because we know that nothing is secretly reaching out and changing a value we depend on elsewhere. In short, functional programming makes it *safe* to optimise performance.

JAVASCRIPT ISN'T A
FUNCTIONAL LANGUAGE

I've heard[1] lots of people debate the merits of functional programming in JavaScript. If you listen to these debates, at some point, you'll hear someone state: "JavaScript isn't a functional programming language." Now, I must admit, I found this confusing when I first heard it. It stumped me, because I didn't see how that statement was relevant to the conversation. What does it matter if JavaScript is or isn't a functional programming language?

As I did more research though, the reason for my confusion became clear. People use this same phrase to make at least three different arguments. What they're trying to say with that phrase depends on the context. Here are the three most common thoughts people try to express by saying JavaScript isn't a functional pro-

---

[1] Well, to be accurate, I've *read* more arguments than I've heard. But I've listened to a good number as well.

gramming language:

1. JavaScript isn't a good teaching language if you're trying to learn functional programming.
2. JavaScripts's language design means that it's missing lots of features that make functional programming convenient and expressive; and
3. Attempting to write code using a functional style in JavaScript is akin to cargo-culting—intellectually incoherent and counterproductive, at best.

We'll examine each of these in turn.

§ 6.1. DON'T CHOOSE JAVASCRIPT IF YOU WANT TO LEARN FUNCTIONAL PROGRAMMING

This argument assumes a hypothetical scenario. That is, we, as humble students, want to learn about functional programming. And, we also imagine that a good way to learn about functional programming would be to learn a new programming language. Thus, we, the humble students, approach a wise sage who is learned in the ways of the Functional. And we pose this question: "Oh great sage, we have heard it said that JavaScript is a functional programming language. If we were to learn JavaScript, would we therefore gain an understanding of functional programming also?"

The great sage responds "No! May it never be! JavaScript is *not* a functional programming language." By which they mean, no, learning JavaScript will not automatically train you in functional programming. And they are quite right.

JavaScript is a multi-paradigm language. So it *allows* us to write code in a functional style. We do things like pass functions around as values, most commonly as callbacks to promises. But when people learn JavaScript, they most often learn to write it in a procedural style. Or in recent times, using a more OOP style. These approaches tend to be common because they're familiar to lots of people—both educators and learners. And JavaScript doesn't get in the way. (Well, not too much). It won't force anyone to grapple with functional concepts.

If you try to learn, say, Haskell or Racket though, it's a different story. You're forced to grapple with functional concepts as soon as you go past "Hello World." (Sometimes even before then). If you persevere and become fluent in one of those languages, then yes, you'll learn lots of functional programming concepts along the way. In that sense, JavaScript is not a functional programming language.

And yet. You're reading this book. It's *about* functional programming in JavaScript. I've spent hours upon hours writing this book. Has it all been a waste of time?

JUST ENOUGH FUNCTIONAL TO BE DANGEROUS

JavaScript has just enough functionality to make functional programming possible. In particular, it has two features that make it work:

1. Functions as data; and
2. Closures.

Functions as data

JavaScript allows us to treat functions like most other data types in the language. That is, we can:

- Assign functions to variables;
- Return a function from another function; and
- Pass functions as arguments to other functions.

To illustrate, let's look at some examples. Suppose we have a function that wraps text in a h1 element:

```
(text) => `<h1>${text}</h1>`
```

We can assign that function to a variable:

```
const h1 = (text) => `<h1>${text}</h1>`;
const h1WithAnotherName = h1;
```

We can return it from another function:

```
const heading = (level) => {
  if (level === 1) {
    return (text) => `<h1>${text}</h1>`;
  }
  throw new Error('No other levels implemented');
};
const h1 = heading(1);
```

And we can pass our function as an argument to another function (or method):

```
const sections = [
  'Arachibutyrophobia',
  'Batrachophobia',
  'Coulrophobia',
];
const headings = sections.map(
  (text) => `<h1>${text}</h1>`;
);
```

This ability to sling functions around as data allows us write code in ways that wouldn't otherwise be possible.

Closures

The second language feature that makes functional programming possible is closures. To explain how they work, imagine we have two functions, but we define one of them inside the other. We'll call them outerFunction() and innerFunction():

```
const outerFunction = (a, b, c) => {
  const i = 0;
  const innerFunction = (x, y, z) => {
    const j = 0;

    // Inside this scope, innerFunction() has access
    // to a, b, c, and i, as well as x, y, z, and j.

    // ...

    // Imagine something useful happens here.
  }

  return innerFunction;
}
```

Inside innerFunction()'s scope it has access to the variables from the parent function's scope. That is, it can make use of a, b, c, and i. And innerFunction() continues to have access to these variables, even after we've called outerFunction() and it's out on its own.

It's the combination of these two language features that makes functional programming possible in JavaScript:

1. Functions as data; and
2. Closures.

These features make currying and partial application possible. And we can use them to drive a whole host of other techniques. (Including re-implementing classes and objects from scratch, if you feel so inclined). They're incredibly powerful.

Powerful as they are though, these language features are still rather primitive. They make functional programming possible, yes. But they don't make it convenient or expressive. For a long time, using functional techniques in JavaScript was tedious. Often, it still is. But the situation changed a lot with ES6. The new language specification included two features that made working with functions much more convenient:

- Fat arrow functions; and
- Rest/spread syntax.

Fat arrow functions

We've been using fat arrow functions throughout this book. Before ES6, any function declaration or function expression required the function keyword. For example:

```
// Function expression:
const itemify = function(item) {
  return `<li>${item}</li>`;
};


// Function declaration:
function listify(items) {
  return `<ul>
```

```
    ${items.map(itemify).join('\n')}
  </ul>`;
}
```

Arrow functions are more concise. But, as the Mozilla documentation points out, they have certain limitations. The arrow function:

- Does not have its own bindings to `this` or `super`, and should not be used as methods.
- Does not have `new.target` keyword.
- Not suitable for `call`, `apply` and `bind` methods, which generally rely on establishing a scope.
- Can not be used as constructors.
- Can not use `yield`, within its body.

Much of the time, these 'limitations' are an advantage. They help keep the code simple. Or, to put it another way, they reduce accidental complexity. Which is a big deal.

One big advantage of fat arrow functions is they make it easy to do currying and partial application. Before fat arrows, to write a curried version of `.filter()`, we had to do something like the following:

```
function filter(predicate) {
  return function(arr) {
    return arr.filter(predicate);
  }
}
```

With fat arrows, it's much more concise:

```
const filter = predicate => arr => arr.filter(predicate);
```

The fat arrow version fits on a single line, and has less 'noise'. There's no curly braces to parse, no indentation to interpret, and no return keyword. There's a lot to like about fat arrows.

REST/SPREAD SYNTAX

Another ES6 feature that made life more convenient for functional programmers is rest/spread syntax. This is, in fact, two separate language features that happen to use the same symbol:

1. Rest parameter syntax makes it convenient to work with *variadic functions*. A variadic function is a function that accepts a variable number of arguments.
2. Spread syntax allows an iterable (like an array) to be expanded in places where you'd otherwise have to list out elements by hand. One of the places we can do this is with arguments to function calls.

Before rest/spread, if I was to write an auto-curry function, it may look like this:[2]

```
function curry(fn) {
  const arity = fn.length;
  return function _curry() {
    var args = Array.prototype.slice.call(arguments, 0);
    if (args.length < arity) {
      return function () {
        _curry.bind.apply(_curry, args);
      }
      return fn.apply(null, args);
    };
  }
```

---

[2] This particular auto-curry implementation, I've adapted from Professor Frisby's Mostly Adequate Guide

```
}
```

Note how we're forced to call .slice() on the special arguments variable to convert it to an array. With fat arrows and rest/spread, the code is a little more succinct:

```
const curry = fn => {
  const _curry = (...args) => (args.length < fn.length)
      ? _curry.bind(null, ...args)
      : fn(...args);
  return _curry;
}
```

And it's not just variadic functions that make rest/spread syntax useful. It's also handy for avoiding object mutations and generally making code more concise. Taken as a whole, recent versions of the ECMAScript standard[3] are much more pleasant to work with. But, when trying to write functional code day-to-day, there's lots of features JavaScript lacks. That is, at least when compared to some other, more 'functional' languages.

THE TEMPTATION PROBLEM

And another problem with learning functional programming in a familiar, multi-paradigm language is the temptation problem. That is, when you have the option, it's tempting to fall back on bad habits when you get stuck. We might not see any way to make our code work without introducing a little side-effect right here... With a language like Haskell, however, you don't have that option. You're forced to go all-in and figure out the 'functional' way to get it done.

---

[3] "Recent versions of the ECMAScript standard..." also known as modern JavaScript.

In summary, no, JavaScript may not be a great language for teaching functional programming. That is, *in the scenario where you're choosing between JavaScript and other languages.* But, what if you're already familiar with JavaScript? It's not so silly to learn functional programming in a language you already know. Furthermore, lots of us have jobs to do. And JavaScript is the tool we have available to do those jobs. More on this later.

§ 6.2. FUNCTIONAL PROGRAMMING IN JAVASCRIPT CAN BE FRUSTRATING

Often, when people state "JavaScript isn't a functional programming language," they're expressing frustration. They're frustrated because they have been coding in another language like Haskell or Clojure. And since then, they've come back to write JavaScript code once more. And they find that JavaScript lacks a slew of features that they'd begun to take for granted. This includes features like:

- Enforced functional purity,
- Sophisticated static type checking, and
- Pattern matching.

If you've become accustomed to these features, losing them will highlight how inconvenient it is to work without them. We'll examine each one in turn.

ENFORCED FUNCTIONAL PURITY

Some languages are designed in such a way that we can't cause any side effects. At least, not without making a special effort or exploiting edge cases. Which may sound odd. After all, network calls, writing to the file system, and rendering UIs are what our computer programs are *for*. And, these languages that enforce functional purity can still do all these things. But they cause *effects* as opposed to *side effects*.

What's the difference? Well, its' all about referential transparency (again). Let's consider an example. Here's some code that is *not* referentially transparent:

```
const getMain = () => document.querySelector('main');
const main = getMain();
```

We say that getMain() is not referentially transparent, because it may not return the same value each time we run it. The document may have a <main> element, or it may not. It depends on the page. And we may even get different <main> elements, depending on where and when we run it. It's an impure function.

What if we changed getMain() though, so that it produced a string?

```
const getMain = () => `document.querySelector('main')`;
```

This is now referentially transparent. We always get the same string back, every time we call it. If we want to, we can even run it using eval().

```
const main = eval(getMain());
```

Now, running eval() would be impure, but that doesn't make our getMain() function impure. We have a pure function that always gives us back the same result.

This isn't so different from having getMain() return a thunk. That would look like so:

```
const getMain = () => () => document.querySelector('main');
```

This version of getMain() is also pure. When we call getMain() it always returns the same result. Sure, the thunk it returns is not a pure function. But calling getMain() will always give us the same result, no matter how often we call it.[4]

We can even take this a step further. To clarify what's going on, we can create a class to represent delayed effects.

```
class Effect {
  constructor(thunk) {
    this.run = thunk;
  }
}
```

And we can change getMain() like so:

```
const getMain = () => new Effect(
  () => document.querySelector('main');
);
```

With this change, if we want to get a <main> element, we first call getMain() and then call .run() on the returned Effect object. But getMain() is a pure function. That is, it's referentially transparent, since it always returns the same value.

We could then add a few methods to our Effect class to make it easier to work with. Some of these methods might even look familiar:

```
class Effect {
  constructor(f) {
    this.run = f;
```

---

[4] Yes, JavaScript will give us back references to two separate memory locations. But both memory locations will contain equivalent functions.

```
  }
  map(g) {
    return new Effect(x => g(this.run(x)));
  }
  join(x) {
    return this.run(x);
  }
  flatMap(g) {
    return new Effect(this.run).map(g).join();
  }
  ap(eff) {
    return eff.map(g => g(this.run()));
  }
}
Effect.of = (val) => new Effect(() => val);
```

With that in place, we can then do things like manipulate the DOM. But everything is walled safely away behind the .run() method. Everything remains perfectly pure until we call .run(). For example:

```
const $ = (selector) => new Effect(
  () => document.querySelector(selector)
);

const getAttr = (attrName) => (el) => new Effect(
  () => el.getAttribute(attrName)
);

const setProp = (propName) => (el) => (val) => new Effect(
  () => {
```

```
      el[propName] = val;
      return el;
  }
);

// setGreeting() is a function inside an effect that
// takes a string and returns another effect.
const setGreeting = $('p.greet')
  .map(setProp('innerHTML'));

const greet = $('input.name')
  .flatMap(getAttr('value'))
  .map(name => `Hello ${name}`)
  .ap(setGreeting)
  .join();

greet.run();
```

You can read more about Effect in Appendix D. There, we take
a deep dive into managing side-effects with structures like Effect.
But, why would anyone bother doing this? How does it benefit our
code or program structure?

Well, the benefit is that we've made our effects explicit. This allows us to keep things referentially transparent. But, in JavaScript,
we pay a high price. This whole Effect thing is clumsy.

In contrast, some languages are designed in such a way that
they have no built-in APIs like document.querySelector(). That
is, no APIs that directly cause side-effects. Instead, all the APIs
return Effects (or something like that). And the whole thing is
designed such that you only get to call .run() once. More precisely,
it's called for you when the main function kicks off. The rest of

the code has to line all the effects up such that running one Effect chains other Effects.

If you're used to firing off effectful API+ calls anywhere you want, this may seem tortuous (or even torturous). But 'functional' languages tend to have built-in conveniences that make working this way straightforward. Dealing with structures like Effect becomes much easier. And instead of the programmer simply exercising lots of discipline, the compiler can guarantee all your functions are referentially transparent. And it's nice. We miss out on this benefit in JavaScript. And some people even argue that as a result, we miss out on *most* of the benefits of functional programming.[5]

Alas, this is not how JavaScript works. And JavaScript will never work this way. But, to be fair, few languages work like this. Even languages people tend to think of as 'somewhat functional'—like Scala, F#, and Clojure—don't have this feature. Hence, it is possible to write functional code in languages that don't enforce purity. But it does require more discipline. And it forces programmers to do work a compiler could be doing for us.

SOPHISTICATED STATIC TYPE CHECKING

Another kind of work a compiler could be doing for us is keeping track of types. JavaScript is a dynamically typed, interpreted language. This means that there's no separate compilation step where the computer can interrupt you. It can't say "Hey, you're going to add a number and an object—that doesn't make sense." Instead, JavaScript tries hard to make our crazy idea work. For example, if I type 3 + { foo: 'bar' } into a JavaScript interpreter, I'll get back 3[object Object]. The interpreter coerces both values to a

---

[5] If you'd like to dig deeper on why people think this, Erik Meijer spells out the argument in detail in his essay *The Curse of the Excluded Middle* https://queue.acm.org/detail.cfm?id=2611829.

string and concatenates them. It's like JavaScript has a pathological aversion to telling anyone their types are wrong.

JavaScript coerces types to make our operations work, no matter how ridiculous. And it's this feature that sometimes causes horror and indignation in experienced programmers coming from other languages. But when it comes to functional programming, the main consequence is that we end up doing all the work. We, the programmers, end up keeping track of types in our heads, instead of the computer doing it for us.

In the last decade or so, lots of people have recognised this as a limitation. Thus we now have tools like TypeScript and Flow. These try to add a layer of type checking on top of JavaScript. I've used both professionally, and I have mixed feelings about them. I have caused bugs in production code that type checking could have prevented. That is, if I been more diligent about hunting down any types in the code I changed. And it's good to have the option of creating disjoint unions.[6] TypeScript and Flow have their advantages. But they're still bolted on to a dynamically typed language that wasn't designed with static types in mind. And so I constantly find myself writing code that I know is correct. But then re-writing it more than once so that the type-checker can understand what I'm doing. As David Khourshid put it:

> TypeScript saves you so much time by preventing many programming mistakes & runtime errors, leaving you more time to do other things such as deciphering & fixing insignificant TypeScript errors[7]

This may not be a bad thing. But, after working with Haskell's sophisticated type system, I can see why people miss it when work-

---

[6] This concept goes by a lot of different names. It's disjoint unions in Flow, and discriminated unions in typescript.
[7] David Khourshid ([@DavidKPiano]) on Twitter, 21 March 2022: https://twitter.com/DavidKPiano/status/1505585090314833922

ing with JavaScript. If you're interested in exploring functional programming with TypeScript, I recommend looking into the popular fp-ts library.[8]

PATTERN MATCHING

Another feature people miss from other programming languages is pattern matching. It's one of those features that appears small and unimportant, but turns out to be incredibly powerful.

Pattern matching is something like a mashup of destructuring syntax with a switch statement. Like a switch statement, it lets us run different code, depending on the value of some expression. But, imagine being able to destructure that variable and use the destructured variables in the code block. Here's an example using some JavaScript-like syntax. Imagine we've made a call to fetch(), grabbing some data, and we need to handle the response, res:

```
const fetchData = async (url) => {
  const res = await fetch(url);
  return match(res) {
    when ({ status: 200, body }): {
      body.json();
    }
    when ({ status: 500, body }): {
      console.warn('Error fetching ${url}:\n${body}');
      retry(url, { backoff: 1000, attempts: 1 });
    }
    when ({ status, headers: { location: newUrl } })
      if (300 <= status && status < 400): {
      fetchData(newUrl);
    }
```

---

[8] fp-ts: https://gcanti.github.io/fp-ts/learning-resources/

```
    else {
      throw new Error('Unknown response status');
    }
  }
};
```

In the example, we match on the `res` variable. If the status attribute is 200, we destructure the `body` attribute and call `.json()` on it. If the status attribute is 500, we log a warning and retry. And if the status is between 300 and 399, we attempt to redirect.

The whole `match` block is an expression. Inside each `when` block, there's an implicit assumption. That is, the last expression evaluated is returned as the value for the whole `match` expression. For example, in the `when` clause (`{ status: 500, body }`), the `match` expression resolves to whatever `retry()` returns.

In languages with static type systems, they often take this a whole step further. They allow you to match on types as well as values. This makes for efficient code when working with sum types like Maybe and Either.[9] It's also fantastic when paired with Finite State Machines (FSMs).

Alas, JavaScript does not have support for pattern matching. (At least, not at the time of writing.) The best we can do at the moment is to write a `switch` statement that matches on `true`. We can then write our matches as boolean expressions. For example, our `fetchData()` code from above might turn into something like the following:

```
const fetchData = async (url) => {
  const res = await fetch(url);
  switch(true) {
```

---

[9] We saw Maybe and Result in Chapter 2.

```
    case (res.status === 200):
      return res.body.json;
    case (res.status === 500):
      console.warn(
        `Error fetching ${url}:\n${res.body}`
      );
      return retry(url, { backoff: 1000, attempts: 1 });
    case (300 <= res.status && res.status < 400):
      return fetchData(res.destination);
    default:
      throw new Error('Unknown response code');
  }

}
```

If you're going to use `switch` like this, do make sure to follow one rule. Make sure that *every* `case` has a `return` statement. Otherwise, you're introducing a side effect. If you do it right, you should never need a `break` keyword. The only exception to the rule is if you're taking advantage of fall-through. But that's an advanced technique.

Using `switch` like this is slightly better than a chain of `if...else` statements. But not by much. The lack of destructuring makes everything more verbose. And there's no help from a compiler to tell us if we've covered all possible status codes. It's a poor substitute for pattern matching, but it's the best we can do for now.

We have some hope though. There's a TC39 proposal for pattern matching,[10] and it looks great. The hypothetical code above is based on examples taken directly from the proposal. I encourage you to check it out and get involved.

---

[10] You ran read about the pattern matching proposal and comment on it at: https://github.com/tc39/proposal-pattern-matching.

We've taken a brief look at some features people miss when coming from other, more 'functional' languages, including:

- Enforced functional purity,
- Sophisticated static type checking, and
- Pattern matching.

These are but a handful of the missing capabilities that make functional programming in JavaScript frustrating. If you work in a language where these features are built-in and idiomatic, it's understandable that you'd find working without them annoying. It's even understandable that someone might take their frustration one step further and declare JavaScript a 'bad' or 'useless' language.

§ 6.3. FUNCTIONAL PROGRAMMING WITH JAVASCRIPT IS A CARGO CULT

Some people get so frustrated with the lack of features in JavaScript that they give up. They declare that people who even try to write JavaScript in a functional style are kidding themselves; cargo-culting. That is, they're going through the motions of doing something that *looks like* functional programming. But, they don't understand what they're doing and don't realise any of the benefits.

It's not hard to see how people end up at this point. As we've seen, JavaScript's support for functional idioms is limited. And worse, we end up doing much of the work that a compiler could be doing for us. We're forced to ensure referential transparency by sheer self-discipline. And hence we lose a lot of guarantees that functional code could otherwise give us. Functional programming in JavaScript is less than ideal.

This raises the question though: What's the alternative? What are we to do instead?

The obvious answer is to use another language—one with better support for functional idioms. And we are spoilt for choice these days. We have a plethora of good options that compile to JavaScript (or WASM) such as:

- PureScript;
- Elm;
- ReScript;
- Haskell via GHCJS; or
- ClojureScript.

If you have the option to use any of these as an alternative to JavaScript, go ahead. But for lots of us, that's not possible. Many of us are employed to work specifically as JavaScript developers. Some of us work on large JavaScript codebases, with millions of lines of code. Converting all that to another language with a different paradigm isn't going to happen. And even on smaller code bases, few have the political power to direct our teams to change languages. In short, lots of us *have* to write JavaScript.

Given that we're writing JavaScript, what do we do then? Do we throw our hands up in the air and write code we know could be better? No. We do the best we can with what we've got. Thus I will bend the language to write as functionally as I can. Because that's the best code I know how to write. And along the way I will make compromises. Often, it will be important that the code be comprehensible to others, even if that means losing some safety or brevity. Other times, I'll have no choice but to use libraries and tools chosen by others. Tools that assume an imperative paradigm. But whatever the situation, I'll write the best code I can *given the circumstances*.

Now, someone may object that almost nobody has a gun pointed at their head. We aren't *forced* to work in JavaScript. And so, a principled programmer can refuse to work on JavaScript projects. If enough people did this, then JavaScript would eventually die out, except as a compiler target for 'better' languages. The world would, in theory, be a better place.

And that may be true. The world may well be a better place if everyone refuses to work on JavaScript projects. But it's not going to happen. For the simple reason that I'm not going to starve my family for the sake of functional programming ideals. The economic reality is that I can find oodles more JavaScript jobs than PureScript and Elm jobs. And, sure, I would love to work in Elm or PureScript all day. But my chances of finding a job in Australia working with those, are slim. (Though, I admit, the chances are not zero either). And even if I did manage to find one, and all my readers did likewise, it still wouldn't matter. Because there's a significant number of JavaScript programmers out there that don't like functional programming. They may be misguided, yes (hence this book). But they're never going to change. Even if everyone who understands functional programming abandons JavaScript.

§ 6.4. HOW TO TALK ABOUT IT

The most practical path forward is to show people a better way. Write code that is demonstrably better because it's written in a functional style. Teach people how to write better code. Write guides, tutorials, and books. Speak at conferences. Help dispel the myths that surround functional programming.

Then people will start to feel the frustrating parts of working with functional code in JavaScript. And as a consequence, more people will investigate some of those 'superior' languages. And we might also gain more support for making JavaScript itself less frustrating.

⁂

In summary, when you hear people say "JavaScript isn't a functional language," they may mean different things. For instance, they may mean that JavaScript isn't a great language for *teaching* functional programming. And if that person wanting to learn has *no* JavaScript experience (or no coding experience at all), that's true. JavaScript is less than ideal for teaching functional programming. But, if the learner knows JavaScript, then it's a different situation. As people learn functional programming, they end up mapping the new concepts onto a languages they already know. (For better or worse). And as we saw, JavaScript is just functional enough to teach many of the basic concepts of functional programming. Sure, it may be clunky, but it works.

For some though, that clunkiness is incredibly frustrating. If you have significant experience working in languages without the clunk, working JavaScript can be almost painful. So when people in this category say "JavaScript isn't a functional programming language," they're expression frustration at this clunkiness.

JavaScript does indeed lack many features that make functional programming convenient, expressive, and safe. So saying "JavaScript isn't a functional programming a language" is understandable, even if it's not helpful. And there's some hope that JavaScript can improve. If browser vendors implement TC39 proposals such as:

- Records and tuples;
- Pattern matching; and
- The pipeline operator.

Even if all of these make their way into the language, the frustration will never go away entirely. But it's unfair to say that functional programming in JavaScript is a cargo cult. That brands everyone who writes JavaScript as ignorant, superstitious, and incompetent. Given that lots of us have little option but to write JavaScript, insulting the intelligence of JavaScript developers isn't helpful. Instead, a better idea would be to help people see the benefits of functional programming. Then, we can all write better code.

FUNCTIONAL
PROGRAMMING IS HARD

The final complaint we'll discuss is that functional programming is hard. And this complaint at least has the virtue of being honest. Many other complaints about functional programming are smoke-screens. They have their true source in this one. Further, I not only sympathise, but agree. Functional programming is hard sometimes. And it's hard in two senses:

1. Functional programming is hard to learn; and
2. Functional programming is hard work in pracice.

Of those two, only the first is a true problem. But we'll examine both ways that functional programming is hard in turn.

Lots of people find functional programming difficult to learn; myself included. And worse still, the difficulty takes them by surprise. It's not something you can pick up by reading a handful of blog posts. Or even a couple of books. I'm embarrassed to admit it, but it's taken me years of effort to understand as much as I do. Yet I still consider myself little more than an advanced beginner. And, to add to my humiliation, I'm well aware that it doesn't need to be this hard.

§ 7.2. THE JARGON PROBLEM

Why is functional programming so difficult to learn? One reason people suggest often, is the jargon. And it's not hard to see why. There's *so* much jargon. And not any old jargon. It's jargon taken from obscure, abstract branches of mathematics. From set theory and category theory. For anyone who struggled with math in school, this kind of thing is going to smell suspicious straight away.

If the jargon is such a problem, why don't we change it then? Over in the oop world, they have plenty of jargon too. But there, at least, the jargon has some kind of metaphorical basis. They use terms like 'Factory' or 'Visitor Pattern.' Or even 'class' or 'object.' The metaphors may not be perfect, but people's brains appear to have an easier time grasping them. But terms like Functor, Monad, and Monoid don't map on to anything people experience outside of coding. Or even *inside* of coding. That is, unless you're a mathematician. Why not make life easier for everyone and give these concepts friendlier names?

People have tried this. And not had much success. For at least two reasons:

1. The standards problem; and

2. The jargon is what it is for a reason.

Figure 7.1: The standards problem, as immortalised in the xkcd comic.[1]

First, *the standards problem*. It's not hard to come up with 'friendlier' names for functional programming concepts. Plenty of people have suggested terms like 'Mappable' for Functor and 'Smushable' for Monoid. These aren't bad names. And I rather like the idea of calling monoids smushables. But the trouble is, these concepts already have agreed names. And as soon as we introduce an alternative nomenclature, we cut people off from resources written using the original nomenclature. If you don't know what the community calls a thing, it's difficult to search for it. This makes relevant tutorials and references hard to find. And finding relevant resources is hard enough as it is. By changing the terms, we trade some short-term gain for long-term pain.

---

[1] 'Standards', https://xkcd.com/927. Randall Munroe (the author of xkcd) kindly states that he is "okay with people reprinting occasional comics (with clear attribution) in publications like books, blogs, newsletters, and presentations." (https://xkcd.com/license.html)

Second, the jargon is not arbitrary. The names come from mathematics. And even though mathematics scares a lot of people, having this connection is a good thing. One of the reasons functional programming is so powerful is because of its basis in math. And it also means that people who want to take a deep dive into the theory don't need to learn *yet another* set of arcane terms.

It's too late to try changing the jargon of functional programming. For better or worse, we're stuck with the set of terms in common use. And besides, jargon is not the true problem. Every field of technical expertise has its terms of art. To people outside the field (and novices), the jargon is always arcane and incomprehensible. This is true, regardless of whether the terms come with friendly metaphors or not. Changing the jargon won't solve the problem.

§ 7.3. THE UNLEARNING PROBLEM

The major reason people find learning functional programming difficult is because they come to it already knowing how to write code. Anecdotally, when people learn to code in a functional paradigm from the beginning, they have less trouble. Because it never occurs to them that not being able to mutate variables is a problem. No, to them, that's how programming works. It's the experienced coders who have trouble unlearning the mutation habit. And not just mutation, but many other tricks and techniques too.

Most of us learn to code in an imperative way. We're taught variables and if-statements and for-loops as the fundamental building blocks. And we learn to break problems down into a sequence of small steps, executed in order. Universities and boot-camps then teach us to use algorithms and data structures that assume an imperative approach. And the problem is, imperative code gets the job done. It works.[2]

It's possible to have a long, lucrative career with this imperative toolset. You'll find imperative code the world over. And lots of it needs fixing, so there's money to be made. The more we work in this paradigm, the better we get at it. And we're rewarded for it. We have an excellent hammer, and we're trained to see nails everywhere.

Then you stumble across functional programming. And at first, it's intriguing. But once you go beyond mapping and reducing arrays, it gets difficult. We keep getting stuck. Sometimes, to even *understand* a problem, we have to think through an imperative solution. It feels like there *ought* to be an elegant functional approach. But it remains out of our reach. And for an experienced programmer, this is humbling—if not downright humiliating. Because the paradigm is so different that it's like learning to code all over again.

Experienced developers (like myself) come to functional programming expecting it to be much like learning another programming language. There's some new syntax to get used to, yeah. And sure, the new language is designed to emphasise certain patterns over others. For example, Java's inheritance model is different from Javascript's. But the control structures are near identical. There's lots of overlap. You can transfer tonnes of problem solving approaches from one language to another. And with each new language you add a handful of new ideas and idioms to your toolkit. You level up and feel great about it.

Then you try functional programming. And straight away, half your problem solving toolkit disappears. The other half, you're told, is radioactive and dangerous—for use in only the direst need, and with copious personal protective equipment. Solving a coding puz-

---

[2] More or less, depending on your definition of 'works.'

zle used to take minutes. Now something 'simple' requires days of thought. You go from a 10× developer to 0.1×.

Meanwhile, the job still needs doing. We have jobs writing apps and building websites. A 99.9% reduction in productivity isn't going to make anyone happy. And it's here that the way we teach functional programming often lets developers down. Because we're bewitched by the beauty of functional programming.

§ 7.4. THE BEAUTY PROBLEM

One of the reasons we love functional programming is its beauty. Pure functions—the foundation of everything—are like purest gold. Both valuable and weighty. But if pure functions are like gold, then the jewel at the centre of the metaphorical crown is algebraic structures. They interweave and interconnect like fine filigree.

The trouble is, algebraic structures are not just abstractions. They're *abstractions of abstractions*. And an abstraction hides details. As developers, we use abstractions to solve problems. They hide differences so we can see commonalities. For example, we use Maybe to deal with empty values. Or Either to represent the possibility of failure. Or Effect to corral our side-effects. They're are all abstractions. Then, algebraic structures show us the commonalities between these abstractions by hiding details. Algebraic structures are super-abstract.

Knowing these structures has potential to turn the coding process on its head. With imperative coding, we tend to work with statements. We write a statement that we think will move us closer to our goal. Then we write another. And another. And we keep on in this fashion until the computer has enough instructions to do our bidding.

And in this imperative mindset, we'll often write the happy path first. Then we'll come back and add some error handling. Then we might refactor because we noticed some duplicated code. As we progress, the code grows organically. And as a consequence, it needs constant pruning to keep it tidy.

Algebraic structures offer a different path. One where we attempt to *understand* our problem first. We do this by 'trying on' algebraic structures to see which ones fit. This is why the laws for algebraic structures are so important. They tell us whether a structure fits our problem. And if we're not used to it, it's hard work trying on structures for size. But when we do find a structure that fits, then the beauty reveals itself. It's like we've *discovered* (rather than written) the solution. Often, it has "the feel of profound inevitability."[3] The code almost writes itself. It's magical.

The trouble is, it takes a lot to get to this point. There's so much prerequisite understanding *and* practice needed before it makes sense. But functional programming enthusiasts are, well, enthusiastic to share this beauty and its benefits. And novices are (understandably) curious about these mysterious monoids and monads. As a result, we end up with 1001 monad tutorials and running jokes about spacesuit burritos. Much confusion ensues.

The problem is, monads and functors and applicatives, by themselves, don't solve specific problems. That's not what they're for. They're for solving whole classes of problems at once. But people learn best when they can work with concrete problems. Abstract problems are too difficult to grasp without the hooks of myriad concrete examples.

It's tools like Maybe, Either, Effect, and Task that solve day-to-day programming problems. Once people are familiar with these

---

[3] Elliott (2009), 'Denotational design with type class morphisms (extended version),' *LambdaPix technical report 2009-01*, March 2009, http://conal.net/papers/type-class-morphisms/type-class-morphisms-long.pdf.

(and can see their usefulness), then it's easier to see the common patterns.

If you are someone who writes or speaks or teaches about functional programming, we need your help. Please try to start with the concrete and work towards the abstract. The beauty will still be there, but we need to help people learn to see it.

§ 7.5. THE SNOBBERY PROBLEM

Speaking of 1001 monad tutorials, functional programming also has an image problem. Much of what's great about functional programming has come out of academia. That has enough problematic correlations on its own. But the problem is compounded by us, the functional programming community. We behave in ways that make people assume we're snobs. Or worse, arrogant jerks.

Now, most people I've met in the functional programming community are helpful, welcoming, and kind. But, I've seen a scenario play out where someone new(ish) to functional programming starts to understand algebraic structures. (Or, more specifically, monads). And, having understood, they want to share their epiphany. Hence, they take to social media and start their explanation with something like the following:

> I know monads *seem* scary, but it's really not that difficult. Here's an analogy that helped me finally get it.

And so they launch into their explanation, using whatever analogy helped their understanding. It could be about how monads are like burritos, or space-suits. The specifics don't matter.

The trouble is, their explanation includes subtle errors. And in response, well-meaning, helpful members of the functional programming community jump in with replies. They've seen these errors before. Worse, they've observed how these errors can stunt understanding down the track. They truly want to help.

The newish explainer, though, feels attacked. Because lots of people are telling them they're wrong, all at once. All they were doing was trying to share something that helped them. They weren't even claiming to be an 'expert' at functional programming. Thus, they reply back.

> Sure, the analogy may not be 100% accurate, but it's still helpful right? Those errors are subtle; small. What's the big deal? I stand by the helpfulness of my analogy.

The well-meaning functional programming community member genuinely wants to help the newcomer understand. Furthermore, the newcomer is making it *more* difficult for others to learn, rather than easier. And so the experienced community member responds again, with a clear, but strongly worded, explanation. Perhaps something like this:

> This analogy has problems and leads to inconsistencies once you start working with more esoteric constructions. It's better not to tie your understanding to a problematic analogy like this. Also, there was a typo in your second code snippet.

What the newcomer *hears* though, is:

YOU ARE INCORRECT! YOUR INTELLIGENCE IS PUNY AND YOU ARE NOT WELCOME IN OUR EXCLUSIVE COMPUTER CLUB.

Both parties mean well. Both sincerely want to help people understand algebraic structures. But both parties come away thinking the other party is a jerk (or bunch of jerks). And the onlookers, for better or worse, tend to sympathise with the underdog. That is, the inexperienced explainer. And this further cements this perception that functional programmers are snobs. A bunch of ivory tower academics who care only about the purity and correctness of ideas. Functional programmers appear to have no regard for the realities of shipping real code or the struggles of sincere learners. It may be a false perception, but it's persistent.[4]

WHAT TO DO?

What can we do about this? The stereotypes about functional programmers are well entrenched. Sometimes they're deserved. We may never shift them entirely. But we *can* try not to make it worse. Alas, this is easier said than done. Because it requires humility.

In the scene I described above, the only chance for a positive outcome is if one or both parties shows some humility. Imagine if the less experienced party were able to respond less defensively:

> Oh no. This kind of analogy really helped me so I thought it would be helpful. But if it causes misunderstandings, that's no good. Do you have another approach for teaching that helps people wrap their heads around this stuff?

If that were the response, I imagine that the conversation would have played out differently.

The more experienced party could also show some humility. Imagine if they took a moment to acknowledge that the explainer was only trying to help:

> Totally understand that this kind of analogy helps you feel like you've got a better handle on it. Lots of people go down this path. But in my experience, it's dangerous. Here's why...

Now, it's true, people are broken in all kinds of weird and wonderful ways. Thus, it could still go badly. But I think it's less likely.

---

[4] This story is based on real life observation. I have personally watched it play out over Twitter threads. But, it's also remarkably similar to a blog post by Brent Yorgey entitled _Abstraction, intuition, and the "monad tutorial fallacy_." https://byorgey.wordpress.com/2009/01/12/abstraction-intuition-and-the-monad-tutorial-fallacy/.

And I'll be the first to admit that staying patient and humble when someone is being stubbornly wrong on the Internet[5] is incredibly difficult. But we have to try.

§ 7.6. FUNCTIONAL PROGRAMMING IS HARD WORK

Not only is functional programming hard work to learn, it's also hard work to *do*. At least, that's how it *feels* (at first). Those of us coming from an imperative background are used to breaking down problems in a certain way. As discussed earlier, we tend to start by focussing on the 'happy path'. We work to understand the problem by *writing code*. But it's code that ignores exceptions and edge cases and invalid input. Only once we've got that happy path working do we come back and consider all those other 'sad paths.'

And this approach works. That is, we write software. We ship it. People use it. And most of the time, it mostly does what we intend. To some extent.

Once we move to a functional paradigm though, that strategy doesn't work quite as well as it used to. Instead, structures like Either, Maybe, Task, and Effect get in the way. It's still possible to focus on the happy path, yes. But we're forced to keep acknowledging:

- Yes, this involves an effect;
- Yes, this could throw an error;
- Yes, this value might be empty;
- Yes, this network call might fail;
- Yes, this function requires an external dependency.

If you're using a type checker like TypeScript, the code won't even compile unless all those structures line up.

---

[5] Obligatory XKCD reference: https://xkcd.com/386/

This is, arguably, a Good Thing. That is, functional programming and algebraic structures won't allow us to be lazy and ignore sad paths, effects, and edge cases. As a result, working in a functional style tends to front-load a lot of work we might otherwise have put off until later. (Or not done at all).

Consequently, this way often *feels* slow. Objectively, we might be making just as much progress as with the imperative happy-path approach. But subjectively, it feels like an intellectual grind. We see less visible progress for the effort we put in. Worse still, it often *looks* like slower progress from the outside too. We all know that those sad paths have to be dealt with eventually. But the imperative programmer can whip up a happy path demo in no time at all. The product owner sees the demo and feels like the task is nearly done. The rest is just 'polishing.' Hence, the impearative programmer looks like they're getting things done. Meanwhile, the functional programmer appears to be faffing around with academic nonsense.

It doesn't matter to the product owner that the imperative demo is full of bugs and assumes perfect network infrastructure. For now, they're comforted by the appearance of progress. And the senior on the team is comfortable with the imperative paradigms. Hence they can point out places where the demo code could be faster, or use a familiar pattern for logging and error handling. The functional code, however, appears impenetrable. Familiar techniques for optimisation won't work. The functional approach doesn't appear to offer any tangible benefits.

This is a real problem. Now, sure, if the hypothetical functional programmer were more experienced, they might be faster. Faster, even, than the imperative developer. And the functional approach *should* result in less runtime errors and require less rework. But those are future benefits. They're not apparent to the outside observer *right now*.

Given all this, it's not hard to see how functional programming gets a bad reputation. From the outside, it looks like functional programming doesn't produce results. Never mind that the buggy imperative code will cause a massive outage in a month's time. They shipped.

This raises the question: Why do we bother?

WHAT'S SO GREAT ABOUT FUNCTIONAL PROGRAMMING (AGAIN)?

If you've read this far, you probably don't need convincing that functional programming is a good idea. And we already discussed this in Chapter 2. But it's worth considering again, why do we bother? This book aims to take a clear-eyed look at the difficulties of functional programming in JavaScript. And, despite much mythology and misinformation, we can see lots of real problems. So we have to ask ourselves: Is it worth it? Are the benefits of functional programming worth the effort and difficulty? And what are these benefits, anyway?

Lots of people have tried to expound the benefits of functional programming, myself included. And we've done so with variable success. The trouble is, much of what people like about functional programming is subjective. Different people like different things, for different reasons. For example, some people like the *experience* of functional programming. For them, a functional approach turns coding into a fascinating logic puzzle. They feel like they're being paid to do brain-teasers all day long.

Other people like functional programming because it's different. They're bored of the way they used to code. Or they simply like the intellectual challenge of doing things a different way. The aspect they like of functional programming is the novelty.

These reasons for liking functional programming come down to personal preference. We like what we like. But can we identify objective benefits to functional programming? Does functional programming produce better code?

If we do a little research, it's easy to find lots of reasons why people think functional programming produces better code. Many of these reasons are hand-wavy and vague. But there are some that are more objective. The best arguments tend to fall into two categories:

1. Functional programming produces more expressive code; and
2. Functional programming increases confidence in our code.

Of the two categories, the first is the weaker argument. So we'll discuss expressivity first.

§ 8.1. FUNCTIONAL PROGRAMMING PRODUCES MORE EXPRESSIVE CODE

We touched on expressivity already in Chapter 3. The reasons this is the weaker argument is that it's mostly based on anecdotal observation. That is, what people say about their experience of coding. I have no empirical data to support these claims. But the anecdotal evidence is consistent and widespread, so it's at least worth discussing.

An anecdote people repeat frequently and consistently is that functional programming produces more 'concise' code. Furthermore, people who take up functional programming also describe their code as becoming more 'elegant'. Both descriptions are important.

Individually, both claims are weak. We all know that shorter code does not equal better code. When we set out to write the shortest solution possible, the code becomes hard to decipher. We might also cut corners, leaving edge conditions unchecked or errors unhandled. Making code shorter often makes it worse.

Functional programmers though, consistently describe functional code as more *elegant*. On it's own, again, this is a weak claim. Elegance is a vague, subjective description. What does it matter if the code is elegant? We software developers care about practical questions like:

- Does it work?
- Is it intelligible?
- Is it easy to maintain?
- Is it easy to delete?[1]

Taken together though, elegance and concision add up to more than the sum of their parts. Few people would call the condensed hieroglyphics produced by a code golf challenge, elegant.[2] Sure, we might admire some of the hacks or techniques applied. But rarely would we call the resulting code elegant. And yet, this is an adjective consistently applied to functional code. Why?

I propose the reason for this is that, functional code is expressive. That is, while concise, it also conveys a great deal about the au-

---

[1] Tef (2016), 'Write code that is easy to delete, not easy to extend', *Programming is terrible*, https://programmingisterrible.com/post/139222674273/how-to-write-disposable-code-in-large-systems, 13 February 2016.
[2] What is code golf? "Code Golf is a game designed to let you show off your code-fu by solving problems in the least number of characters." https://code.golf

thor's intent. Functional programming leads to information-dense code.

How does it do this? Well, in an imperative paradigm, we tend to work with statements. That is, a series of instructions that we give to the computer instructing it what to do. Functional programming, though, deals mainly with *expressions*. That is, computations that resolve to a value. In imperative programming, we write one statement after another. But with functional programming, we tend to *compose* expressions using pure functions.

Why does this make a difference? Well, since functional code tends to compose functions and expressions, it uses fewer control structures. Instead, the code tends to use a variety of pure utility functions, composed together to produce more pure functions. And then we compose these pure functions together to produce the final program. Where imperative programming sequences a small set of control structures to organise code, functional programming composes a larger set of utility functions. And each utility function tells us more about the author's intent. This results in more information-dense code. Or, to put it another way, the code is more expressive.

Someone might be thinking, that's just another way of saying that functional code is more 'declarative.' That is, functional code tends to describe *what* we want to do, rather than spelling out every detail of *how* to get the job done. For example, in functional programming, we tend to prefer using .map(), .filter(), and .reduce() over for...each loops. The array methods are more declarative because they say *what* we want done, not how.

This is a fair point. Functional code does tend to be more declarative. The trouble is, *everyone* is trying to write declarative code. It doesn't matter whether they're a functional programmer or not. It's entirely possible to write declarative code with an OOP+ or imperative approach. For example, imagine we were writing some kind of to-do application. We might write a method like the one below:

```
class ToDoApp {

    // Constructor and other methods go here

    reconnect() {
        this.connectToDB();
        const remoteTasks = this.fetchRemoteTasks();
        this.reconcile(remoteTasks);
        this.emit('render');
    }

    // ...

}
```

The author of this code can legitimately claim that it's declarative. This `reconnect()` method doesn't spell out every little detail of what needs to be done. And a functional version might not look so very different:

```
const reconnect = (localTasks) =>
    connectToDB()
        .chain(fetchRemoteTasks)
        .map(reconcile(localTasks))
        .chain(render);
```

On the surface, the two versions resemble each other. They follow roughly the same series of steps. Both are 'declarative.' But the functional version is more expressive. That is, it conveys more

information about how this code fits together. For example, the
.chain() and .map() methods tell us that connectToDB() returns
a monad. Given the context, we can probably infer that it's something like an Effect. The .chain() calls tell us that fetchRemote-
Taks() and render() return a structure that's the same type as
what connectToDB() returns. We can also tell that fetchRemote-
Taks() requires a DB connection, since it chains immediately after connectToDB(). All of this information is hidden in the OOP+
version. Yet both can legitimately be called 'declarative.'

When we say that functional code is more expressive, we mean
that it conveys more information about the author's intent. It does
this because functional code tends to be built out of small, compos-
able utility functions. Because we prefer pure functions, both the
functions themselves, and the way they are composed, are meaningful. This tends to produce concise, elegant code (though not
always). And the information available may not be obvious to all,
since readability is a function of familiarity. But it's still there.

§ 8.2. FUNCTIONAL PROGRAMMING GIVES US MORE CONFIDENCE IN
OUR CODE

While expressivity is great, you'll notice we have to hedge a lot
when we talk about it. We use phrases like 'in general' and 'tends
to'. We can't say that *all* functional code is *always* more expressive,
all the time. Because it's not. And if this was the *only* benefit
of functional programming, perhaps it's not worth the effort. But
there are benefits to functional programming that are always true.
We can say with certainty that functional programming gives us
more confidence in our code.

If you talk to functional programmers though, you won't often
hear them express it this way. Instead, you may hear them say that

functional programming lets us *reason* about our code. And to people outside the functional programming community, this sounds strange. Who would write code that you can't think about? Nobody does that.

Functional programmers have something specific in mind when they talk about 'reasoning about code.' They're not talking about thinking in general. No, they're talking about the consequences that flow from working only with pure functions.

As we discussed in Chapter 4, a pure function is referentially transparent. That is, if we call the function with some set of inputs, it will always produce the same output. We can even take this one step further. If you replace the function call with its output, the resulting calculation should still end up with the same result. In short, pure functions produce consistent results.

This consistency allows us to start making deductions about how our code will behave. For example, let's imagine we have some function f(), and calling f() with x results in a:

```
f(x) === a // true
```

Then suppose we have some other function, g(), and we call g() with the result of f(x). The following should always be true:[3]

```
g(f(x)) === g(a) // true
```

And I hope at least some of you reading this are rolling your eyes and thinking "Well duh. Of course that's how it works." This is obvious stuff, right?

What happens though if we give our functions and variables different names. Like the following:

---

[3] We'll ignore the fact that f() and g() might return identical objects, for the moment.

- What if we rename `f()` to `connectToDB()`?
- And change a to conn?
- And `g()` to `selectRecentTasks()`?
- And x to `config`?

Would that change our expectations?

```
// g(f(x)) === g(a) becomes...
selectRecentTasks(connectToDB(config)) ===
    selectRecentTasks(conn) // ????
```

Would we expect this to hold true, 100% of the time?
What if we wrote it like this:

```
const conn = connectToDB(config);
const tasksA = selectRecentTasks(connectToDB(config));
setTimeout(
    () => {
        tasksB = selectRecentTasks(conn);
        tasksA === tasksB // ?????
    },
    60000
);
```

If we're working with pure functions, the answer is 'yes.' We would still expect tasksA to be the same as tasksB. Though, perhaps we wouldn't write database queries this way. And furthermore, tasksA and tasksB may not have the *type* you might expect.

Consider our `reconnect()` example from earlier. Both the OOP and functional version contained a `reconcile()` step. We'll assume that this step merges the local tasks with the remote list. If we consider the functional version, we could list a number of properties we might expect to be true:

- `reconcile(a, b).length <= a.length + b.length`
  We don't end up with more tasks than we started with.
- `reconcile(a, b).length >= Math.max(a.length, b.length)`
  We don't lose any tasks.
- `reconcile(a, []) === a`
  Reconciling with an empty list doesn't change anything.
- `reconcile([], b) === b`
  Reconciling with an empty list doesn't change anything (on either side).
- `reconcile(a, b).every(t => a.map(x => x.id).includes(t.id)`
  `|| b.map(x => x.id).includes(t.id)) === true`
  Every task in the reconciled list came from one of the input lists.

If we wanted, we could write property tests[4] to assert that these properties hold. But that's not really the point. The point is that we can think about these properties more easily because the output of `reconcile()` depends *only* on its two inputs. There are no hidden mutable properties that might change the output.

Once we're confident with those properties, we can then make inferences about how this function will interact with other code. For example, we might look at the third and fourth properties and see some performance improvements. That is, if we receive an empty array, return the other array—no need to process any further.

Now, someone might argue "Hey! I can do all that same reasoning with an OOP version. There's nothing special going on here." And that's true. We're not saying functional code is the only code anyone can ever think about. Rather, we're saying that pure functions are *easier* to reason about.

With a method attached to an object, the result might depend

---

[4] For more on property tests, see https://jrsinclair.com/articles/2021/how-to-get-started-with-property-based-testing-in-javascript-with-fast-check/

on some mutable internal state. Or perhaps the method loads its data from localStorage. Perhaps it scrapes the DOM to build a new list of current tasks. We don't know. We'd have to read the code to find out.

And that's the point.

A pure function's behaviour depends only on its inputs. This makes pure functions easier to reason about because of all the things we know it's *not* doing. It makes them easier to test, because there's much less need to mock out a special environment for the code to run in. We only have to generate appropriate inputs.

Pure functions are easier to debug. All the data relevant to the function is listed in its signature. We don't have to go spelunking through the code to see if there's a global variable buried there. We don't have to go searching to see if it's fetching data from another source. As long as the input values stay the same, the output value will not change. Not ever.

It's this unchangeableness that gives us greater confidence in our code. Because, if I have a pure function, and I verify that it works for a given set of inputs, I know that it will *always* work for that set of inputs. If I truly have a pure function, it will never change behaviour because some other part of the code changed.

Its the combination of these two benefits that makes functional programming worth the effort:

1. We get more expressive code;
2. That we have more confidence in.

Even though functional programming feels like more work at times, the benefits outweigh the costs. And that's why, is spite of the many frustrations, functional programming in *JavaScript* is worth the effort.

Throughout this book, we've looked at a bunch of complaints:

- We've considered how some people feel functional programming makes code unreadable;
- We've examined performance concerns with both recursion and immutable data;
- We've discussed the concerns functional programmers themselves have with JavaScript; and
- We talked about how, for many of us, learning functional programming is difficult.

In this chapter, we considered whether it's worth it. If there are so many problems with functional programming in JavaScript, why do we bother? We bother because functional programming gives us two benefits that make it worthwhile:

1. Expressivity; and
2. Confidence.

The question is, though, faced with so many difficulties, what do we *do*?

To answer that, I think it's worth stepping back and thinking about our profession. What do software developers get paid for?

Well, we write code.

Why do we do that?

We write code to deliver business value of some sort. We build web applications and developer tooling and open-source libraries. And we build these things to help other people get stuff done. We get paid to write code because it delivers value to someone, somewhere.

We only deliver value, though, to the degree that our code does what it's supposed to. When it doesn't, we call this a bug. Now, bugs vary in severity. Some cause whole applications or products to fail. Others are mere annoyances. But they all get in the way of that value flowing.

Bugs are best exterminated by preventing them from hatching in the first place. To do that, we turn to tools and techniques that give us more confidence in our code. They help us confirm our expectation that the code does what we intend.

Functional programming isn't the only tool that helps us with this. We turn to tools like testing and type checkers too. But functional programming plays particularly well with both those things. And it helps in its own right.

Sometimes, though, we have to make tradeoffs. There's no point in writing perfect code that never ships. Code that doesn't ship provides zero business value.[5] If our team members refuse to merge our PR, we don't ship. If a senior rewrites our code from scratch, that delays shipping. If we're falling into endless debates about code style, we're not writing code. Which also means we're not shipping. Hence, we make tradeoffs.

How do we know which tradeoffs to make, though? Are there places where we need to push back? How do we know?

Back in Chapter 3, we talked about adjusting our code style to suit the familiarity of the team. This is a tradeoff. But note that in those examples, we always traded expressivity for familiarity. We didn't compromise on confidence. We kept our functions pure. And hence the core functionality remained constant.

In real life, things aren't always quite so simple. On rare occasions, we may compromise our confidence, so we can ship. Sometimes, deadlines and commercial pressures make this a necessity. But those times ought to be rare. For most situations, we can write

---

[5] Okay, yes. There's *some* value in unshipped code. We learn. We may avoid mistakes we would otherwise have made. But those benefits are tangential to helping our users get stuff done.

a clear order of preference:

1. Compromise on personal code style preferences first;
2. Compromise on expressivity second; and
3. Compromise confidence only as a last resort.

This order of priorities can help guide our discussions, as well as our code. And if we hold the line on confidence, then we will spend less time fixing bugs. That leaves more time to help others see how elegant and expressive functional code can be. Once they understand how it works, that is. And I sincerely hope this book goes some way to helping you do that.

PART II
APPENDICES

WHAT ARE HIGHER-ORDER FUNCTIONS, AND WHY WOULD ANYONE CARE?

"Higher-order function" is one of those phrases people throw around a lot. But it's rare for anyone to stop to explain what that means. Perhaps you already know what a higher-order function is. But how do we use them in the real world? What are some practical examples of when and how they're useful? Can we use them for manipulating the DOM? Or, are people who use higher-order functions showing off? Are they over-complicating code for no good reason?

I happen to think higher order functions are useful. In fact, I think they are one of the most important features of JavaScript as a language. But before we get on to that, let's start by breaking down what a higher-order function is. To get there, we start with functions as variables.

In JavaScript, we have at least three different ways of writing a new function.[1] First, we can write a *function declaration*. For example:[2]

```
// Take a DOM element and wrap it in a list item element.
function itemise(el) {
    const li = document.createElement('li');
    li.appendChild(el);
    return li;
}
```

I hope that's familiar. But, you probably know we could also write it as a *function expression*. That might look like so:

```
const itemise = function(el) {
    const li = document.createElement('li');
    li.appendChild(el);
    return li;
}
```

And then, there's yet another way to write the same function: As an *arrow function*:

---

[1] There's more than three ways to write a function, but we can talk about that another time.

[2] If you're more experienced with functional programming, you may have noticed I've used impure functions and some... verbose function names. This isn't because I don't know about impure functions or general functional programming principles. And it's not how I would write function names in production code. This is an educational piece, so I've tried to choose practical examples that beginners will understand. Sometimes that means making compromises. You can read more about functional purity in [Appendix 5][#how-to-deal-with-dirty-side-effects-in-your-pure-functional-javascript].

```
const itemise = (el) => {
    const li = document.createElement('li');
    li.appendChild(el);
    return li;
}
```

For our purposes, all three functions are essentially the same. [3] But notice that the last two examples assign the function to a variable. It seems like such a small thing. Why *not* assign a function to a variable? But this is a Big Deal. Functions in JavaScript are 'first class'. That is, we can:

- Assign functions to variables;
- Pass functions as arguments to other functions; and
- Return functions from other functions. [4]

That's nice, but what does this have to do with higher-order functions? Well, pay attention to those last two points. We'll come back to them in a moment. Meanwhile, let's look at some examples.

We've seen assigning functions to variables. What about passing them as parameters though? Let's write a function that we can use with DOM elements. If we run `document.querySelectorAll()` we get back a `NodeList` rather than an array. `NodeList` doesn't have a `.map()` method like arrays do, so let's write one:

```
// Apply a given function to every item in a NodeList and
// return an array.
function elListMap(transform, list) {
```

---

[3] This is not always true. All three ways of writing functions have subtle differences in practice. The differences are to do with what happens to the magic this keyword and labels in stack traces.

[4] Wikipedia contributors (2019). 'First-class citizen,' *Wikipedia, the free encyclopedia*, viewed 19 June 2019, https://en.wikipedia.org/wiki/First-class_citizen.

```
    // list might be a NodeList, which doesn't have .map(),
    // so we convert it to an array.
    return [...list].map(transform);
}


// Grab all the spans on the page with the class 'for-listing'
const mySpans = document.querySelectorAll('span.for-listing');

// Wrap each one inside an <li> element. We re-use the
// itemise() function from earlier.
const wrappedList = elListMap(itemise, mySpans);
```

In this example, we pass our itemise function as an argument to the elListMap function. But we can use our elListMap function for more than creating lists. For example, we might use it to add a class to a set of elements.

```
function addSpinnerClass(el) {
    el.classList.add('spinner');
    return el;
}


// Find all the buttons with class 'loader'
const loadBtns = document.querySelectorAll('button.loader');

// Add the spinner class to all the buttons we found.
elListMap(addSpinnerClass, loadBtns);
```

Our elLlistMap function takes a function as a parameter, transform. This means we can re-use the elListMap function to do a bunch of different tasks.

We've now seen an example of passing functions as parameters. But what about returning a function from a function? What might that look like?

Let's start by writing a regular old function. We want to take a list of <li> elements and wrap them in a <ul>. Not so difficult:

```
function wrapWithUl(children) {
    const ul = document.createElement('ul');
    return [...children].reduce((listEl, child) => {
        listEl.appendChild(child);
        return listEl;
    }, ul);
}
```

But what about if we later on have a bunch of paragraph elements we want to wrap in a <div>? No problem. We write a function for that too:

```
function wrapWithDiv(children) {
    const div = document.createElement('div');
    return [...children].reduce((divEl, child) => {
        divEl.appendChild(child);
        return divEl;
    }, div);
}
```

This will work fine. But those two functions are looking mighty similar. The only meaningful thing that changes between the two is the parent element we create.

Now, we *could* write a function that takes two parameters: the type of parent element, and the list of children. But, there is another way to do it. We could create a function that returns a function. It might look something like this:

```
function createListWrapperFunction(elementType) {
    // Straight away, we return a function.
    return function wrap(children) {
        // Inside our wrap function, we can 'see' the
        // elementType parameter.
        const parent = document.createElement(elementType);
        return [...children].reduce((parentEl, child) => {
            parentEl.appendChild(child);
            return parentEl;
        }, parent);
    }
}
```

Now, that may look a little complicated at first, so let's break it down. We've created a function that does nothing but return another function. But, the returned function *remembers* the elementType parameter. Then, later, when we call the returned function, it knows what kind of element to create. So, we could create wrapWithUl and wrapWithDiv like so:

```
const wrapWithUl = createListWrapperFunction('ul');
// Our wrapWithUl() function now 'remembers' that it creates
// a ul element.

const wrapWithDiv = createListWreapperFunction('div');
// Our wrapWithDiv() function now 'remembers' that it creates
// a div element.
```

This business where the returned function 'remembers' something has a technical name. We call it a *closure*. [5] Closures are excessively handy, but we won't worry too much about them right now.

So, we've seen:

- Assigning a function to a variable;
- Passing a function as a parameter; and
- Returning a function from another function.

All in all, having first-class functions seems pretty good. But what does this have to do with *higher-order* functions? Well, let's see the definition of higher-order function.

§ A.2. WHAT IS A HIGHER-ORDER FUNCTION?

A higher-order function is:

> A function that takes a function as an argument, or returns a function as a result[6]

Sound familiar?   In JavaScript, functions are first-class citizens. The phrase 'higher-order functions' describes functions which take advantage of this.   There's not much to it.   It's a fancy-sounding phrase for a simple concept.

§ A.3. EXAMPLES OF HIGHER-ORDER FUNCTIONS

Once you start looking though, you'll see higher-order functions all over the place. The most common are functions that accept

---

[5] If you'd like to learn more about closures, try Master the JavaScript Interview: What is a Closure? by Eric Elliott:
https://medium.com/javascript-scene/master-the-javascript-interview-what-is-a-closure-b2f0d2152b36

[6] *Higher Order Function* (2014), viewed 19 June 2019, http://wiki.c2.com/?HigherOrderFunction.

functions as parameters. So we'll look at those first. Then we'll go through some practical examples of functions that return functions.

FUNCTIONS THAT ACCEPT FUNCTIONS AS PARAMETERS

Anywhere you pass a 'callback' function, you are using higher-order functions. These are everywhere in front-end development. One of the most common is the `.addEventListener()` method. We use this when we want to make actions happen in response to events. For example, if I want to make a button pop up an alert:

```
function showAlert() {
  alert(
    'Fallacies do not cease to be fallacies because they' +
    ' become fashions'
  );
}

document.body.innerHTML +=
'<button type="button" class="js-alertbtn">
  Show alert
</button>';

const btn = document.querySelector('.js-alertbtn');

btn.addEventListener('click', showAlert);
```

In this example, we create a function that shows an alert. Then we add a button to the page. And finally, we pass our `showAlert()` function as an argument to `btn.addEventListener()`.

We also see higher-order functions when we use array iteration

172 | *What are higher-order functions, and why would anyone care?*

methods. That is, methods like `.map()`, `.filter()`, and `.reduce()`. We already saw this with our `elListMap()` function:

```
function elListMap(transform, list) {
    return [...list].map(transform);
}
```

Higher-order functions also help us deal with delays and timing. The `setTimeout()` and `setInterval()` functions both help us manage *when* functions execute. For example, if we wanted to remove a highlight class after 30 seconds, we might do something like this:

```
function removeHighlights() {
    const els = document.querySelectorAll('.highlighted');
    elListMap(el => el.classList.remove('highlighted'), els);
}

setTimeout(removeHighlights, 30000);
```

Again, we create a function and pass it to another function as an argument.

As you can see, we use functions that accept functions often in JavaScript. In fact, you probably use them already.

FUNCTIONS THAT RETURN FUNCTIONS

Functions that return functions aren't as common as functions that accept functions. But they're still useful. One of the most helpful examples is the `maybe()` function. I've adapted this one from Reginald Braithewaite's *JavaScript Allongé*.[7] It looks like

---

[7] Reginald Braithewaite, *JavaScript Allongé, the "Six" Edition:* https://leanpub.com/javascriptallongesix/read

this:

```
function maybe(fn) {
  return function _maybe(...args) {
    // Note that the == is deliberate.
    if ((args.length === 0) || args.some(a => (a == null))) {
      return undefined;
    }
    return fn.apply(this, args);
  }
}
```

Rather than decode how it works right now, let's look first at how we might use it. Let's examine our function elListMap() again:

```
// Apply a given function to every item in a NodeList and
// return an array.
function elListMap(transform, list) {
  // list might be a NodeList, which doesn't have .map(),
  // so we convert it to an array.
  return [...list].map(transform);
}
```

What happens if we pass a null or undefined value in to elListMap() by accident? We get a TypeError and whatever we were doing comes crashing to a halt. The maybe() function lets us fix that. We use it like this:

```
const safeElListMap = maybe(elListMap);
safeElListMap(x => x, null);
// ← undefined
```

Instead of everything crashing to a halt, the function returns undefined. And if we were to pass that into another function protected by maybe()... it would return undefined again. And we can keep on using maybe() to protect any number of functions we like. Much simpler than writing a bazillion if-statements.

Functions that return functions are also common in the React community. For example, connect() from react-redux is a function that returns a function.

§ A.4. SO WHAT?

We've seen some individual examples of what higher-order functions can do. But so what? What do they give us that we wouldn't have without them? Is there something bigger here than a handful of contrived examples?

To answer that question, let's examine one more example. Consider the built-in array method .sort(). It has its problems, yes. It mutates the array instead of returning a new one. But let's ignore that for a second. The .sort() method is a higher-order function. It takes a function as one of its parameters.

How does it work? Well, if we want to sort an array of numbers, we first create a comparison function. It might look something like this:

```
function compareNumbers(a, b) {
    if (a === b) return 0;
    if (a > b)   return 1;
    /* else */   return -1;
}
```

Then, to sort the array, we use it like so:

```
let nums = [7, 3, 1, 5, 8, 9, 6, 4, 2];
nums.sort(compareNumbers);
console.log(nums);
// ] [1, 2, 3, 4, 5, 6, 7, 8, 9]
```

We can sort a list of numbers. But how useful is that? How often do we have a list of numbers that need sorting? Not so often. If I need to sort something, it's more often an array of objects. Something more like this:

```
let typeaheadMatches = [
    {
        keyword: 'bogey',
        weight: 0.25,
        matchedChars: ['bog'],
    },
    {
        keyword: 'bog',
        weight: 0.5,
        matchedChars: ['bog'],
    },
    {
        keyword: 'boggle',
        weight: 0.3,
        matchedChars: ['bog'],
    },
    {
        keyword: 'bogey',
        weight: 0.25,
        matchedChars: ['bog'],
    },
```

```
        {
            keyword: 'toboggan',
            weight: 0.15,
            matchedChars: ['bog'],
        },
        {
            keyword: 'bag',
            weight: 0.1,
            matchedChars: ['b', 'g'],
        }
    ];
```

Imagine we want to sort this array by the weight of each entry. Well, we *could* write a new sorting function from scratch. But we don't need to. Instead, we create a new comparison function.

```
function compareTypeaheadResult(word1, word2) {
    return -1 * compareNumbers(word1.weight, word2.weight);
}

typeaheadMatches.sort(compareTypeaheadResult);
console.log(typeaheadMatches);
// ] [
//   {keyword: "bog", weight: 0.5, matchedChars: ["bog"]},
//   ...
// ]
```

We can write a comparison function for any kind of array we want. The .sort() method makes a deal with us. It says: "If you can give me a comparison function, I will sort any array. Don't worry about what's in the array. If you give me a comparison function, I'll sort it." So we don't have to worry about writing a sorting algorithm ourselves. We focus on the much more simple task of comparing two elements.

Now, imagine if we didn't have higher-order functions. We could not pass a function to the .sort() method. We would have to write a new sorting function any time we needed to sort a different kind of array. Or, we'd end up re-inventing the same thing with function pointers or objects. Either way would be much clumsier.

We do have higher-order functions though. And this lets us separate the sorting function from the comparison function. Imagine if a clever browser engineer came along and updated .sort() to use a faster algorithm. Everyone's code would benefit, regardless of what's inside the arrays they're sorting. And there's a whole collection of higher-order array functions that follow this pattern.

That brings us to the broader idea. The .sort() method *abstracts* the task of *sorting* away from what's *in* the array. We have what we call a 'separation of concerns'. Higher-order functions let us create abstractions that would be clumsy or impossible otherwise. And creating abstractions is 80% of software engineering.

Whenever we refactor our code to remove repetition, we're creating abstractions. We see a pattern, and replace it with an abstract representation of that pattern. As a result, our code becomes more concise and easier to understand. At least, that's the idea.

Higher-order functions are a powerful tool for creating abstractions. And there's a whole field of mathematics related to abstractions. It's called *Category Theory*. To be more accurate, Category Theory is about finding abstractions of abstractions. To put it another way, it's about finding patterns of patterns. And over the last 70 years or so, clever programmers have been stealing their ideas. These ideas show up as programming language features and libraries. If we learn these patterns of patterns, we can sometimes remove whole swathes of code. Or reduce complex problems down to elegant combinations of simple building blocks. Those building blocks are higher-order functions. And this is why higher-order functions are important. Because with them, we have another powerful tool to fight complexity in our code.

If you'd like to learn more about higher-order functions, here's some references:

- Higher-Order Functions: Chapter 5 of *Eloquent JavaScript* by Marijn Haverbeke:
  `https://eloquentjavascript.net/05_higher_order.html`
- Higher Order Functions: Part of the *Composing Sofware* series by Eric Elliott: `https://medium.com/javascript-scene/`
- Higher-Order Functions in JavaScript by M. David Green for Sitepoint:
  `https://www.sitepoint.com/higher-order-functions-javascript/`

You're probably using higher-order functions already. JavaScript makes it so easy for us that we don't think about them much. But it's handy to know what people are talking about when they throw around the phrase. It's not so complicated. But behind that one small idea, there's a lot of power.

THE MARVELLOUSLY
MYSTERIOUS JAVASCRIPT
MAYBE MONAD

You finally made it. You stepped through the looking glass. You learned functional programming. You mastered currying and composition, and followed the path of functional purity. And gradually, you notice a change in the attitude of the other programmers. There's ever-so-slightly less disdain in their voice when you talk to them. Every so often you'll get a little nod when you happen to mention immutable data structures. You've begun to earn their respect. And yet...

There's something they won't talk about. When they think you're not in earshot, every so often, you'll overhear the word 'monad' discussed in hushed tones. But as soon as they notice you're there, they change the subject. One day, you pluck up the courage to ask someone. "What's this monad thing I keep hearing about?" The other programmer just looks at you. After an awkward silence she simply says "I can't talk about it." So you ask another programmer and she replies "Maybe when you've learned Haskell." She walks away sadly, shaking her head.

Mystified, you start searching for answers on the Internet. And at first there seems to be plenty of people eager to explain the mysterious monads. But, there's a problem. It's as if every single one of them writes in some kind of code. They talk about applicative functors, category theory, algebraic structures and monadic laws. But none of them seem to explain what monads are for. What do they do? Why do they exist? You keep searching and discover article after article trying to come up with some kind of analogy. Monads are like tupperware. Monads are like trees. Monads are like a bucket line. Monads are like hazmat suits. Monads are like burritos. Comparing monads to burritos considered harmful... It starts to drive you mad.

One day, one of the more junior programmers approaches you, a furtive expression on his face. "Look, you've got to stop asking questions about monads, okay? It upsets people. Monads are cursed. It's not that people don't want to tell you about them. They can't." He looks around again and continues in a hushed tone. "Even ol' father Crockford couldn't break the curse. He tried. In a keynote conference talk and everything. But it got him. He couldn't do it. Either you figure monads out or you don't. No one can help you. That's just how it works."

Monads have a bad reputation in the JavaScript community. Douglas Crockford once said that monads are cursed. Once you finally understand monads, you lose the ability to explain monads to others.[1] Even experienced functional programmers treat monads with respect. And some of the explanations out there *are* hard to understand. Especially if they dive straight into category theory. But, if you can understand Promises then you can understand monads.

In this chapter we will look at just one type of monad: The Maybe monad. Focussing on just one will help explain the basic idea without getting too bogged down in theory. Hopefully it will be enough to set you on the path to enlightenment. I'm still new to Monads myself. Perhaps new enough that the curse hasn't fully taken hold. Let's see how it goes...

§ B.1. A QUICK RECAP OF PROMISES

In the olden days (before jQuery 3.x), you would often see people make an AJAX call like this:

```
Promise.resolve($.getJSON('/path/to/my/api'))
    .then(function(data) {
```

_____

[1] Monads and Gonads (YUIConf Evening Keynote),
https://www.youtube.com/watch?v=dkZFtimgAcM

```
    // Do something with the data in here.
  });
```

Promise.resolve() was necessary because jQuery's version of Promises didn't fully meet the Promises/A+ standard. So, clever people would use the .resolve() method to make the jQuery version into a real Promise.

Now, if I wanted to, I could rewrite the code above so that it uses a named function instead of an anonymous function:

```
function doSomething(data) {
    // Do something with the data in here.
}


Promise.resolve($.getJSON('/path/to/my/api'))
    .then(doSomething);
```

Same code, just in a different order.

Now, one of the features that makes promises so popular is that you can chain them together. So if I have a few named functions, I can chain them up like so:

```
Promise.resolve($.getJSON('/path/to/my/api'))
    .then(doSomething)
    .then(doSomethingElse)
    .then(doAnotherThing);
```

This is neat and tidy, but let's rewrite the code above to make it clearer what's going on:

```
var p1 = Promise.resolve($.getJSON('/path/to/my/api'));
var p2 = p1.then(doSomething);
var p3 = p2.then(doSomethingElse);
var p4 = p3.then(doAnotherThing);
```

Here we are creating four promises. Each one represents a future value. The intermediate variables aren't necessary, but they make things clearer. Each `.then()` call is returning a new promise object. The key thing is that the functions themselves don't have to know that they're inside a Promise. They just expect regular values as parameters. This is good because it keeps the functions simple and easy to understand.

Now, if you've worked with Promises before, then you may know that `Promise.resolve()` can work with plain values too, not just AJAX calls. So, returning to the example above, we could swap `$.getJSON()` with a plain old object:

```
var data = {foo: 'bar'};
Promise.resolve(data)
    .then(doSomething)
    .then(doSomethingElse)
    .then(doAnotherThing);
```

This creates a promise that resolves straight away with the value of `data`. What's interesting to note here is that for this code to work with a regular value instead of an asynchronous value, *we didn't change a thing*. All the named functions still take regular variables and return whatever they return.

Monads are like Promises in that they allow us to handle tricky things with a consistent approach. 'Tricky things' might include asynchronous data, or null values, or something else entirely.The monad hides away a bunch of the complexity so we don't have to think about it. This lets us concentrate on writing simple, pure functions that are easy to understand.

To show how a monad might be useful, let's consider an example problem. Let's say we're working on some code to personalise a website. We want to change the main banner of the site depending on what province (or state) the user lives in. Most of the time, the user data looks something like this:

```
var user = {
    email: 'james@example.com',
    accountDetails: {
        address: {
            street:    '123 Fake St',
            city:      'Exampleville',
            province:  'NS',
            postcode:  '1234'
        }
    },
    preferences: {}
}
```

And we have banner images stored in a map like so:

```
var banners = {
    'AB': '/assets/banners/alberta.jpg',
    'BC': '/assets/banners/british-columbia.jpg',
    'MB': '/assets/banners/manitoba.jpg',
```

```
    'NL': '/assets/banners/newfoundland-labrador.jpg',
    'NS': '/assets/banners/nova-scotia.jpg',
    'NT': '/assets/banners/northwest-territories.jpg',
    'ON': '/assets/banners/ontario.jpg',
    'PE': '/assets/banners/prince-edward.jpg',
    'QC': '/assets/banners/quebec.jpg',
    'SK': '/assets/banners/saskatchewan.jpg',
    'YT': '/assets/banners/yukon.jpg',
};
```

So, for the 'ordinary' case, we can write a nice simple function to grab the right banner:

```
function getUserBanner(banners, user) {
    return banners[user.accountDetails.address.province];
}
```

One line. Simple. Easy. Done.

And because we're badass functional programmers, we could even write this mostly pointfree (with a little help from the Ramda library):

```
var R       = require('ramda'),
    compose = R.compose,
    prop    = R.prop,
    path    = R.path;

var getUserBanner = compose(
    prop(R.__, banners),
    path(['accountDetails', 'address', 'province'])
);
```

Except...

Sometimes the user might not have logged in. In that case the user variable looks like this:

```
var user = {};
```

So, to handle that case, we abandon pointfree style, and add a check to see if the accountDetails exist:

```
function getUserBanner(banners, user) {
    if (typeof user.accountDetails !== 'undefined') {
        return banners[user.accountDetails.address.province];
    }
}
```

And sometimes, the server throws an error, and it that case the user variable looks like this:

```
var user = null;
```

So, to handle that case we add another condition:

```
function getUserBanner(banners, user) {
    if (user !== null) {
        if (user.accountDetails !== undefined) {
            return banners[
                user.accountDetails.address.province
            ];
        }
    }
}
```

But there's also the case where the user has signed in, but has never filled out their address details. In that case the user variable looks like this:

```
var user = {
    email:              'james@example.com',
    accountDetails: {}
};
```

So we need another condition to check that there is an address:

```
function getUserBanner(banners, user) {
    if (user !== null) {
        if (user.accountDetails !== undefined) {
            if (user.accountDetails.address !== undefined) {
                return banners[
                    user.accountDetails.address.province
                ];
            }
        }
    }
}
```

This is starting to look like a pyramid of doom. To make it slightly better, could merge it all into one if-statement:

```
function getUserBanner(banners, user) {
    if ((user !== null)
        && (user.accountDetails !== undefined)
        && (user.accountDetails.address !== undefined)) {
        return banners[user.accountDetails.address.province];
    }
}
```

But this isn't a great improvement on the pyramid of doom. What was an easy one-line function has transformed into a messy bunch of conditionals. It's hard to read and makes the purpose of the function less clear. Fortunately, the Maybe monad can help us.

§ B.3. THE MAYBE MONAD

In essence, a monad is simply a wrapper around a value. We can create that with an object that holds a single property:

```
var Maybe = function(val) {
    this.__value = val;
};


var maybeOne = new Maybe(1);
```

Typing that new keyword everywhere is a pain though (and has other problems). It would be nice to have a shortcut like Promise.resolve(). So we create a class method of():

```
Maybe.of = function(val) {
    return new Maybe(val);
};


var maybeOne = Maybe.of(1);
```

Because the point of our Maybe monad is to protect us from empty values (like null and undefined), we'll write a helper method to test the value in our Maybe:

```
Maybe.prototype.isNothing = function() {
    return (
        this.__value === null ||
        this.__value === undefined
    );
};
```

So far, our Maybe wrapper doesn't do anything for us. If anything, it makes life harder. We want to be able to do things with the value. So, we write a method that will let us get the value and do something with it. But we'll also put a guard on it, to protect us from those pesky null and undefined values. We'll call the method map, since it maps from one value to another.[2]

```
Maybe.prototype.map = function(f) {
    if (this.isNothing()) {
        return Maybe.of(null);
    }
    return Maybe.of(f(this.__value));
};
```

This is already enough to be useful. We can rewrite our getUser-Banner() function so that it uses a Maybe to protect us from empty values:

```
function getUserBanner(banners, user) {
    return Maybe.of(user)
        .map(prop('accountDetails'))
        .map(prop('address'))
```

---

[2] This implementation of map is based on the Maybe monad found in *Professor Frisby's Mostly Adequate Guide to Functional Programming* by Brian Lonsdorf.

```
        .map(prop('province'))
        .map(prop(R.__, banners));
}
```

If any of those `prop` calls returns undefined then Maybe just skips over it. We don't have to catch or throw any errors. Maybe just quietly takes care of it.

This looks a lot like our Promise pattern. We have something that creates the monad, `Maybe.of()`, rather like `Promise.resolve()`. And then we have a chain of `.map()` methods that do something with the value, rather like `.then()`. A Promise lets us write code without worrying about whether data is asynchronous or not. The Maybe monad lets us write code without worrying whether data is empty or not.

§ B.4. MAYBE OF A MAYBE? MAYBE NOT.

Now, what if we got excited about this whole Maybe thing, and decided to write a function to grab the banner URL? We could return a Maybe for that function too:

```
var getProvinceBanner = function(province) {
    return Maybe.of(banners[province]);
};
```

With that done, we can add it in to our `getUserBanner()` function:

```
function getUserBanner(user) {
    return Maybe.of(user)
```

```
        .map(prop('accountDetails'))
        .map(prop('address'))
        .map(prop('province'))
        .map(getProvinceBanner);
}
```

But now we have a problem. Instead of returning a Maybe with a string inside it, we get back a Maybe with another Maybe inside it. To do something with the value, I would have to add a map inside a map:

```
getUserBanner(user)
    .map(function(m) {
        m.map(function(banner) {
            // I now have the banner,
            // but this is too many maps
        }
    })
```

We're back to another pyramid of doom. We need a way of flattening nested Maybes back down—*join* them together, you might say. So we create a .join() method that will unwrap an outer Maybe if we have them double-wrapped:

```
Maybe.prototype.join = function() {
    return this.__value;
};
```

This lets us flatten back to just one layer. So we can add in the join to getUserBanner():

```
function getUserBanner(user) {
    return Maybe.of(user)
        .map(prop('accountDetails'))
        .map(prop('address'))
        .map(prop('province'))
        .map(getProvinceBanner)
        .join();
}
```

That gets us back to one layer of Maybe. So we can work with functions that pass back Maybes. But, if we're mapping and joining a lot, we might as well combine them into a single method. It allows us to *chain* together functions that return Maybes:

```
Maybe.prototype.chain = function(f) {
    return this.map(f).join();
};
```

Now, using .chain(), our function has one less step:

```
function getUserBanner(user) {
    return Maybe.of(user)
        .map(R.prop('accountDetails'))
        .map(R.prop('address'))
        .map(R.prop('province'))
        .chain(getProvinceBanner);
}
```

And because Ramda's path() handles missing values in a sensible way, we can reduce this down even further:

```
function getUserBanner(user) {
    return Maybe.of(user)
        .map(path(['accountDetails', 'address', 'province']))
        .chain(getProvinceBanner);
}
```

With chain() we now have a way of interacting with functions that return other Maybe monads. Notice that with this code, there's no if-statements in sight. We don't need to check every possible little thing that might be missing. If a value is missing, the next step just isn't executed.

§ B.5. BUT WHAT DO YOU *DO* WITH IT?

You may be thinking, "That's all well and good, but my banner value is still wrapped up inside a Maybe. How do I get it out again?" And that's definitely a legitimate question. But let me ask you another question first: "Do you *need* to get it out?"

Think about it for a moment. When you wrap a value up inside a Promise, you *never* get it out again. The event loop moves on, and you can never come back to the context you started with.[3] Once you wrap the value in the Promise, you never unwrap it. And it's just fine. We work inside callback functions to do what we need to do. It's not a big deal.

Unwrapping a Maybe kind of defeats the purpose of having it at all. Eventually though, you will want to do *something* with your value. And we need to decide what to do if the value is null at that point. With our example, we will want to add our banner to the DOM. What if we wanted to have a fallback banner to use if we get

---

[3] OK. OK. Yes, with async/await and generators you can kind-of do something that looks like that, but you definitely can't with ES5. And yet we still managed to get things done before we had all this syntactic sugar.

back an empty Maybe? For this we'll need one more little method:[4]

```
Maybe.prototype.orElse = function(default) {
    if (this.isNothing()) {
        return Maybe.of(default);
    }

    return this;
};
```

Now, if our visiting user happens to come from Nunavut, we can at least show *something*. And since we've got that sorted, let's also grab the banner element from the DOM. We'll wrap it up in a Maybe too, since it's possible someone could change the HTML on us.

```
// Provide a default banner with .orElse()
var bannerSrc = getUserBanner(user)
            .orElse('/assets/banners/default-banner.jpg');

// Grab the banner element and wrap it in a Maybe too.
var bannerEl = Maybe.of(
    document.querySelector('.banner > img')
);
```

Now we have two Maybes: bannerSrc and bannerEl. We want to use them both together to set the banner image (our original problem). Specifically, we want to set the src attribute of the DOM element in bannerEl to be the string inside bannerSrc. What if we wrote a function that expected two Maybes as inputs?

---

[4] Note this implementation of .orElse() differs from other libraries. This one expects you to return a regular value, while others expect you to wrap the return value in a Maybe yourself.

```
var applyBanner = function(mBanner, mEl) {
    mEl.__value.src = mBanner.__value;
    return mEl;
};


applyBanner(bannerSrc, bannerEl);
```

This would work just fine, until one of our values was null. Because we're pulling values out directly, we're not checking to see if the value is empty. It defeats the entire purpose of having things wrapped in a Maybe to start with. With .map(), we have a nice interface where our functions don't need to know anything about Maybe. Instead, they just deal with the values they're passed. If only there was some way to use .map() with our two Maybes...

Let's rewrite our applyBanner() as if we were just working with regular values:[5]

```
var curry = require('ramda').curry;

var applyBanner = curry(function(el, banner) {
    el.src = banner;
    return el;
});
```

Note that we've curried the function. Now, what happens if we run .map() with applyBanner()?

```
bannerEl.map(applyBanner);
// => Maybe([function])
```

---

[5] Yes, this function is impure and mutates data, but we'll ignore that for now.

We get a *function* wrapped in a Maybe. Now, stay with me. This isn't as crazy as it might seem. The basic building block of functional programming is first-class functions. And all that means is that we can pass functions around just like any other variable. So why not stick one inside a Maybe? All we need then is a version of .map() that works with a Maybe-wrapped function. In other words, a method that *applies* the wrapped function to our Maybe with a value. We'll call it .ap for short:

```
Maybe.prototype.ap = function(someOtherMaybe) {
    return someOtherMaybe.map(this.__value);
}
```

Remember that in the context above, this.__value is a function. So we're using map the same way we have been all along—it just applies a normal function to a Maybe. Putting it together we get:

```
var mutatedBanner = bannerEl.map(applyBanner).ap(bannerSrc);
```

This works, but isn't super clear. To read this code we have to remember that applyBanner takes two parameters. Then also remember that it's partially applied by bannerEl.map(). And then it's applied to bannerSrc. It would be nicer if we could say "Computer, I've got this function that takes two regular variables. Transform it into one that works with Maybe monads." And we can do just that with a function called liftA2 ('2' because we have two parameters):

```
var liftA2 = curry(function(fn, m1, m2) {
    return m1.map(fn).ap(m2);
});
```

Note that we assume fn is curried. We now have a neat function that can take another function and make it work with our Maybes:

```
var applyBannerMaybe = liftA2(applyBanner);
var mutatedBanner     = applyBannerMaybe(bannerEl, bannerSrc);
```

Mission accomplished. We're now able to pluck the province value from deep within the user preference object. We can use that to look up a banner value, and then apply it to the DOM, safely, without a single if-statement. We can just keep mapping and chaining without a care in the world. Using Maybe, I don't have to think about all the checks for null. The monad takes care of that for me.

§ B.6. POINTFREE STYLE

Now, at this point you may be thinking "Hold on just a second there, Sir. You keep talking about functional programming, but all I see is objects and methods. Where's the function composition?" And that is a valid objection. But we've been writing functional JavaScript all along, just using a different style. We can transform all these methods into plain functions easily:

```javascript
// map :: Monad m => (a -> b) -> m a -> m b
var map = curry(function(fn, m) {
    return m.map(fn);
});


// chain :: Monad m => (a -> m b) -> m a -> m b
var chain = curry(function(fn, m) {
    return m.chain(fn);
});


// ap :: Monad m => m (a -> b) -> m a -> m b
var ap = curry(function(mf, m) { // mf, not fn, because this
                                 // is a wrapped function
    return mf.ap(m);
});


// orElse :: Monad m => m a -> a -> m a
var orElse = curry(function(val, m) {
    return m.orElse(val);
});
```

With that done, we can write the whole thing in a more point-free style:

```javascript
var pipe        = require('ramda').pipe;
var bannerEl    = Maybe.of(
    document.querySelector('.banner > img')
);
var applyBanner = curry(function(el, banner) {
```

```
    el.src = banner; return el;
});


// customiseBanner :: Monad m => String -> m DOMElement
var customiseBanner = pipe(
    Maybe.of,
    map(R.path(['accountDetails', 'address', 'province'])),
    liftA2(applyBanner, bannerEl)
);


customiseBanner(user);
```

There are still two impure functions, but customiseBanner is now pointfee. And here's were things start to get interesting...

Note that when we defined the functional forms of map, chain, ap etc. we didn't include any mention of Maybe. This means that any object that implements .map() can work with the map function. Any object that implements .chain() can work with chain. And so on. Imagine if we had other objects that implemented these methods...

§ B.7. PIPELINES

To show how this works, I'm going to break all the rules for a moment. I'm going to alter the Promise prototype. Note that this is being performed by a trained professional under controlled conditions. Do not try this at home:

```
Promise.of             = Promise.resolve;
Promise.prototype.map   = Promise.prototype.then;
Promise.prototype.chain = Promise.prototype.then;
```

```
Promise.prototype.ap    = function(otherPromise) {
    return this.then(otherPromise.map);
};
```

With this done, I can now do things like this:

```
// Set the innerHTML attribute on an element.
// Note, this method mutates data. Use with caution.
var setHTML = curry(function (el, htmlStr) {
    el.innerHTML = htmlStr;
    return el;
});


// Get an element.
// Note, this is an impure function because it relies on the
// global document. Use with caution.
var getEl = compose(Promise.of, document.querySelector);


// Fetch an update from a server somewhere.
// Takes a URL and returns a Promise for JSON.
var fetchUpdate = compose(Promise.of, $.getJSON);


// Process an update.
var processUpdate = pipe(
    map(R.path(['notification', 'message'])),
    liftA2(setHTML, getEl('.notifications'))
);


var updatePromise = fetchUpdate('/path/to/update/api');
processUpdate(updatePromise);
```

Take a moment to look at that processUpdate function again.

We've defined a pipeline that takes a monad input and then map and lift to transform it. But there's nothing in the pipeline that assumes we're working with a Promise. The pipeline would work just as well with our Maybe monad. And, in fact, it would work with any object that meets the Fantasyland Monad Spec.

So, let's recap what we've looked at:

- A monad is like a Promise in that you don't act on a value directly. Instead, we use map to apply a callback, just like then with Promises.
- The Maybe monad will only map if it has a value. So, when we map a Maybe, we don't have to worry about null or undefined values.
- If we use monad libraries that conform to a specification, we can compose pipelines. These pipelines can work interchangeably with different types of monad.

§ B.8. FURTHER READING

There is a lot more to learn about monads, and there are many other types of monads besides Maybe. I encourage you to keep reading and find out more. There are three main resources I've found helpful:

- *Professor Frisby's Mostly Adequate Guide to Functional Programming* by Brian Lonsdorf
- *The Perfect API* by James Forbes
- *The Fantasyland Specification* sets out rules that keep monads and other algebraic structures interoperable.
- *A Map to Success: Functors in Javascript* by Kevin Welcher (a functor is just an object that implements map(), so monads are functors that implement a couple of extra things on top).

*
**

Slowly, it begins to make sense. You wouldn't claim to 'understand' monads, but you can see how using Maybe might save a lot of effort. So, you slip it in to your next commit, neatly avoiding a couple of null checks. You don't make a big deal about it. The other programmers don't say anything, but you know that they noticed. There's still a lot to learn, but monads are no longer a complete mystery. They're tools for getting a job done.

ELEGANT ERROR HANDLING WITH THE JAVASCRIPT EITHER MONAD

Let's talk about how we handle errors for a little bit. In JavaScript, we have a built-in language feature for dealing with exceptions. We wrap problematic code in a `try...catch` statement. This lets us write the 'happy path' in the `try` section, and then deal with any exceptions in the `catch` section. And this is not a bad thing. It allows us to focus on the task at hand, without having to think about every possible error that might occur. It's definitely better than littering our code with endless if-statements.

Without `try...catch`, it gets tedious checking the result of every function call for unexpected values. Exceptions and try...catch blocks serve a purpose. But, they have some issues. And they are not the only way to handle errors. In this article, we'll take a look at using the 'Either monad' as an alternative to try...catch.

A few things before we continue. In this chapter, we'll assume you already know about function composition and currying. If you need a minute to brush up on those, that's totally OK. And a word of warning. If you haven't come across things like monads before, they might seem really... different. Working with tools like these takes a mind shift. And that can be hard work to start with.

Don't worry if you get confused at first. Everyone does. I've listed some other references at the end that may help. But don't give up. This stuff is intoxicating once you get into it.

§ C.1. A SAMPLE PROBLEM

Before we go into what's wrong with exceptions, let's talk about why they exist. There's a reason we have things like exceptions and try...catch blocks. They're not all bad all of the time.

To explore the topic, we'll attempt to solve an example problem. I've tried to make it at least semi-realistic. Imagine we're writing a function to display a list of notifications. We've already managed (somehow) to get the data back from the server. But, for whatever reason, the back-end engineers decided to send it in CSV format rather than JSON. The raw data might look something like this:

```
timestamp,content,viewed,href
2018-10-27T05:33:34+00:00,@madhatter invited you to tea,unread,https://
2018-10-26T13:47:12+00:00,@queenofhearts mentioned you in 'Croquet Tourn
2018-10-25T03:50:08+00:00,@cheshirecat sent you a grin,unread,https://e
```

Now, eventually, we want to render this code as HTML. It might look something like this:

```
<ul class="MessageList">
  <li class="Message Message--viewed">
    <a
      href="https://example.com/invite/tea/3801"
      class="Message-link">
      @madhatter invited you to tea
    </a>
    <time datetime="2018-10-27T05:33:34+00:00">
      27 October 2018
    </time>
  <li>
  <li class="Message Message--viewed">
    <a
      href="https://example.com/discussions/croquet/1168"
      class="Message-link">
      @queenofhearts mentioned you in 'Croquet Tournament'
      discussion
    </a>
    <time datetime="2018-10-26T13:47:12+00:00">
      26 October 2018
    </time>
  </li>
  <li class="Message Message--viewed">
    <a
      href="https://example.com/interactions/grin/88"
      class="Message-link">
      @cheshirecat sent you a grin
    </a>
    <time datetime="2018-10-25T03:50:08+00:00">
      25 October 2018
    </time>
```

```
    </li>
</ul>
```

To keep the problem simple, for now, we'll just focus on process-ing each line of the CSV data. We start with a few simple functions to process the row. The first one will split a line of text into fields:

```
function splitFields(row) {
    return row.split('","');
}
```

Now, this function is over-simplified because this is a tutorial. Our focus is on error handling, not CSV parsing. If there was ever a comma in one of the messages, this would go horribly wrong. Please do not ever use code like this to parse real CSV data. If you ever *do* need to parse CSV data, please use a well-tested CSV parsing library.

Once we've split the data, we want to create an object. And we'd like each property name to match the CSV headers. Let's assume we've already parsed the header row somehow. (We'll cover that bit in a moment.) But we've come to a point where things might start going wrong. We have an error to handle. We throw an error if the length of the row doesn't match the header row. (_.zipObject is a lodash function).

```
function zipRow(headerFields, fieldData) {
    if (headerFields.length !== fieldData.length) {
        throw new Error(
            "Row has an unexpected number of fields"
        );
    }
```

```
        return _.zipObject(headerFields, fieldData);
}
```

After that, we'll add a human-readable date to the object, so
that we can print it out in our template. It's a little verbose, as
JavaScript doesn't have awesome built-in date formatting support.
And once again, we encounter potential problems. If we get an invalid date, our function throws an error.

```
function addDateStr(messageObj) {
    const errMsg =
        'Unable to parse date stamp in message object';
    const months = [
        'January', 'February', 'March', 'April', 'May',
        'June', 'July', 'August', 'September', 'October',
        'November', 'December'
    ];
    const d = new Date(messageObj.datestamp);
    if (isNaN(d)) {
        throw new Error(errMsg);
    }

    const datestr = [
        d.getDate(), months[d.getMonth()], d.getFullYear(),
    ].join(' ');
    return {datestr, ...messageObj};
}
```

And finally we take our object, and pass it through a template
function to get an HTML string.

```
const rowToMessage = _.template(
'<li class="Message Message--<%= viewed %>">
  <a href="<%= href %>" class="Message-link">
   <%= content %>
  </a>
  <time datetime="<%= datestamp %>"><%= datestr %></time>
<li>');
```

If we end up with an error, it would also be nice to have a way to print that too:

```
const showError = _.template(
    '<li class="Error"><%= message %></li>'
);
```

And once we have all of those in place, we can put them together to create our function that will process each row.

```
function processRow(headerFieldNames, row) {
    try {
        fields = splitFields(row);
        rowObj = zipRow(headerFieldNames, fields);
        rowObjWithDate = addDateStr(rowObj);
        return rowToMessage(rowObj);
    } catch(e) {
        return showError(e);
    }
}
```

So, we have our example function. And it's not too bad, as far as JavaScript code goes. But let's take a closer look at how we're managing exceptions here.

So, what's good about `try...catch`? The thing to note is, in the above example, any of the steps in the `try` block might throw an error. In `zipRow()` and `addDateStr()` we intentionally throw errors. And if a problem happens, then we simply catch the error and show whatever message the error happens to have on the page. Without this mechanism, the code gets really ugly. Here's what it might look like without exceptions. Instead of throwing exceptions, we'll assume that our functions will return `null`.

```
function processRowWithoutExceptions(headerFieldNames, row) {
    fields = splitFields(row);
    rowObj = zipRow(headerFieldNames, fields);
    if (rowObj === null) {
        return showError(new Error(
            'Encountered a row with an unexpected number ' +
            'of items'
        ));
    }

    rowObjWithDate = addDateStr(rowObj);
    if (rowObjWithDate === null) {
        return showError(new Error(
            'Unable to parse date in row object'
        ));
    }

    return rowToMessage(rowObj);
}
```

As you can see, we end up with a lot of boilerplate if-statements. The code is more verbose. And it's difficult to follow the main logic.

Also, a null value doesn't tell us very much. We don't actually know why the previous function call failed. So, we have to guess. We make up an error message, and call showError(). Without exceptions, the code is messier and harder to follow.

But look again at the version *with* exception handling. It gives us a nice clear separation between the 'happy path' and the exception handling code. The try part is the happy path, and the catch part is the sad path (so to speak). All of the exception handling happens in one spot. And we can let the individual functions tell us why they failed. All in all, it seems pretty nice. In fact, I think most of us would consider the first example a neat piece of code. Why would we need another approach?

§ C.3.   PROBLEMS WITH TRY...CATCH EXCEPTION HANDLING

The good thing about exceptions is they let you ignore those pesky error conditions. But unfortunately, they do that job a little too well. You just throw an exception and move on. We can work out where to catch it later. And we all intend to put that try...catch block in place. Really, we do. But it's not always obvious where it should go. And it's all too easy to forget one. And before you know it, your application crashes.

Another thing to think about is that exceptions make our code impure. Why functional purity is a good thing is a whole other discussion. But let's consider one small aspect of functional purity: referential transparency. A referentially-transparent function will always give the same result for a given input. But we can't say this about functions that throw exceptions. At any moment, they might throw an exception instead of returning a value. This makes it more complicated to think about what a piece of code is actually doing. But what if we could have it both ways? What if we could come up with a pure way to handle errors?

Pure functions always return a value (even if that that value is nothing). So our error handling code, needs to assume we always return a value. So, as a first attempt, what if we returned an Error object on failure? That is, wherever we were throwing an error, we return it instead. That might look something like this:

```
function processRowReturningErrors(headerFieldNames, row) {
    fields = splitFields(row);
    rowObj = zipRow(headerFieldNames, fields);
    if (rowObj instanceof Error) {
        return showError(rowObj);
    }

    rowObjWithDate = addDateStr(rowObj);
    if (rowObjWithDate instanceof Error) {
        return showError(rowObjWithDate);
    }

    return rowToMessage(rowObj);
}
```

This is not much of an improvement on the version without exceptions. But it is better. We've moved responsibility for the error messages back into the individual functions. But that's about it. We've still got all of those if-statements. It would be really nice if there was some way we could encapsulate the pattern. In other words, if we know we've got an error, don't bother running the rest of the code.

So, how do we do that? It's a tricky problem. But it's achievable with the magic of *polymorphism*. If you haven't come across polymorphism before, don't worry. All it means is 'providing a single interface to entities of different types.'[1] In JavaScript, that means we create objects that have methods with the same name and signature. But we give them different behaviours. A classic example of this is application logging. We might want to send our logs to different places depending on what environment we're in. What if we created two logger objects, like so?

```javascript
const consoleLogger = {
    log: function log(msg) {
        console.log(
            'This is the console logger, logging:',
            msg
        );
    }
};


const ajaxLogger = {
    log: function log(msg) {
        return fetch(
            'https://example.com/logger',
            {method: 'POST', body: msg}
        );
    }
};
```

Both objects define a log function that expects a single string

---

[1] Stroustrup, B., 2012, Bjarne Stroustrup's C++ Glossary

parameter. But they behave differently. The beauty of this is that we can write code that calls .log(), but doesn't care which object it's using. It might be a consoleLogger or an ajaxLogger. It works either way. For example, the code below would work equally well with either object:

```
function log(logger, message) {
    logger.log(message);
}
```

Another example is the .toString() method on all JS objects. We can write a .toString() method on any class that we make. So, perhaps we could create two classes that implement .toString() differently. We'll call them Left and Right (I'll explain why in a moment).

```
class Left {
  constructor(val) {
    this._val = val;
  }
  toString() {
    const str = this._val.toString();
    return `Left(${str})`;
  }
}

class Right {
  constructor(val) {
    this._val = val;
  }
  toString() {
```

```
    const str = this._val.toString();
    return `Right(${str})`;
  }
}
```

Now, let's create a function that will call `.toString()` on those two objects:

```
function trace(val) {
    console.log(val.toString());
    return val;
}

trace(new Left('Hello world'));
// ] Left(Hello world)

trace(new Right('Hello world'));
// ] Right(Hello world);
```

Not exactly mind-blowing, I know. But the point is that we have two different kinds of behaviour using the same interface. That's polymorphism. But notice something interesting. How many if-statements have we used? Zero. None. We've created two different kinds of behaviour without a single if-statement in sight. Perhaps we could use something like this to handle our errors...

§ C.6. LEFT AND RIGHT

Getting back to our problem, we want to define a happy path and a sad path for our code. On the happy path, we just keep happily running our code until an error happens or we finish. If we end up on the sad path though, we don't bother with trying to run the code any more. Now, we could call our two classes 'Happy' and 'Sad' to represent two paths. But we're going to follow the naming conventions that other programming languages and libraries use. That way, if you do any further reading it will be less confusing. So, we'll call our sad path 'Left' and our happy path 'Right' just to stick with convention.

Let's create a method that will take a function and run it if we're on the happy path, but ignore it if we're on the sad path:

```
/**
 * Left represents the sad path.
 */
class Left {
    constructor(val) {
        this._val = val;
    }
    runFunctionOnlyOnHappyPath() {
        // Left is the sad path. Do nothing
    }
    toString() {
        const str = this._val.toString();
        return `Left(${str})`;
    }
}


/**
 * Right represents the happy path.
 */
class Right {
  constructor(val) {
```

```
    this._val = val;
  }
  runFunctionOnlyOnHappyPath(fn) {
    return fn(this._val);
  }
  toString() {
    const str = this._val.toString();
    return `Right(${str})`;
  }
}
```

Then we could do something like this:

```
const leftHello  = new Left('Hello world');
const rightHello = new Right('Hello world');


leftHello.runFunctionOnlyOnHappyPath(trace);
// does nothing



rightHello.runFunctionOnlyOnHappyPath(trace);
// ) Hello world
// ← "Hello world"
```

MAP

We're getting closer to something useful, but we're not quite there
yet. Our .runFunctionOnlyOnHappyPath() method returns the _val
property. That's fine, but it makes things inconvenient if we want
to run more than one function. Why? Because we no longer know
if we're on the happy path or the sad path. That information is
gone as soon as we take the value outside of Left or Right. So, what

we can do instead, is return a Left or Right with a new _val inside. And we'll shorten the name while we're at it. What we're doing is mapping a function from the world of plain values to the world of Left and Right. So we call the method map():

```
/**
 * Left represents the sad path.
 */
class Left {
    constructor(val) {
        this._val = val;
    }
    map() {
        // Left is the sad path
        // so we do nothing
        return this;
    }
    toString() {
        const str = this._val.toString();
        return `Left(${str})`;
    }
}
/**
 * Right represents the happy path
 */
class Right {
    constructor(val) {
        this._val = val;
    }
    map(fn) {
        return new Right(
```

```
            fn(this._val)
        );
    }
    toString() {
        const str = this._val.toString();
        return `Right(${str})`;
    }
}
}
```

With that in place, we can use Left or Right with a fluent style syntax:

```
const leftHello       = new Left('Hello world');
const rightHello      = new Right('Hello world');
const helloToGreetings = str =>
    str.replace(/Hello/, 'Greetings,');

leftHello.map(helloToGreetings).map(trace);
// Doesn't print any thing to the console
// ← Left(Hello world)

rightHello.map(helloToGreetings).map(trace);
// ] Greetings, world
// ← Right(Greetings, world)
```

We've effectively created two tracks. We can put a piece of data on the right track by calling new Right() and put a piece of data on the left track by calling new Left().

If we map along the right track, we follow the happy path and process the data. If we end up on the left path though, nothing happens. We just keep passing the value down the line. If we were to say, put an Error in that left track, then we have something very

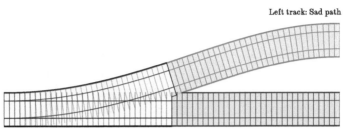

Left track: Sad path

Right track: Happy path

Figure C.1: Each class represents a track. The left track is our sad path, and right track is the happy path. Also, I've totally stolen this railway metaphor from Scott Wlaschin.

similar to `try...catch`.

As we go on, it gets to be a bit of a pain writing 'a Left or a Right' all the time. So we'll refer to the Left and Right combo together as 'Either'. It's *either* a Left or a Right.

SHORTCUTS FOR MAKING EITHER OBJECTS

So, the next step would be to rewrite our example functions so that they return an Either. A Left for an Error, or a Right for a value. But, before we do that, let's take some of the tedium out of it. We'll write a couple of little shortcuts. The first is a static method called `.of()`. All it does is return a new Left or Right. The code might look like this:

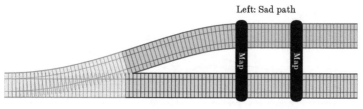

Left: Sad path

Right: Happy path

Figure C.2: We use .map() to move us along the track.

```
Left.of = function of(x) {
    return new Left(x);
};


Right.of = function of(x) {
    return new Right(x);
};
```

To be honest, I find even `Left.of()` and `Right.of()` tedious to write. So I tend to create even shorter shortcuts called `left()` and `right()`:

```
function left(x) {
    return Left.of(x);
}
```

```
function right(x) {
    return Right.of(x);
}
```

With those in place, we can start rewriting our application functions:

```
function zipRow(headerFields, fieldData) {
    const lengthMatch = (
        headerFields.length == fieldData.length
    );
    return (!lengthMatch)
        ? left(new Error("Unexpected number of fields"))
        : right(_.zipObject(headerFields, fieldData));
}


function addDateStr(messageObj) {
    const errMsg = 'Unable to parse date in message object';
    const months = [
        'January', 'February', 'March', 'April', 'May',
        'June', 'July', 'August', 'September', 'October',
        'November', 'December'
    ];
    const d = new Date(messageObj.datestamp);
    if (isNaN(d)) { return left(new Error(errMsg));  }

    const datestr = [
        d.getDate(), months[d.getMonth()], d.getFullYear(),
    ].join(' ');
    return right({datestr, ...messageObj});
}
```

The modified functions aren't so very different from the old ones. We just wrap the return value in either Left or Right, depending on whether we found an error.

That done, we can start re-working our main function that processes a single row. We'll start by putting the row string into an Either with right(), and then map splitFields to split it:

```
function processRow(headerFields, row) {
    const fieldsEither   = right(row).map(splitFields);
    // ...
}
```

This works just fine, but we get into trouble when we try the same thing with zipRow():

```
function processRow(headerFields, row) {
    const fieldsEither  = right(row).map(splitFields);
    const rowObj = fieldsEither.map(
        zipRow /* wait. this isn't right */
    );
    // ...
}
```

This is because zipRow() expects two parameters. But functions we pass into .map() only get a single value from the ._val property. One way to fix this is to create a curried version of zipRow(). It might look something like this:

```
function zipRow(headerFields) {
    return function zipRowWithHeaderFields(fieldData) {
        const lengthMatch = (
```

```
        headerFields.length == fieldData.length
    );
    return (!lengthMatch)
        ? left(new Error("Unexpected number of fields"))
        : right(_.zipObject(headerFields, fieldData));
    };
}
```

This slight change makes it easier to transform `zipRow` so it will work nicely with `.map()`:

```
function processRow(headerFields, row) {
    const fieldsEither = right(row).map(splitFields);
    const rowObj       = fieldsEither.map(
        zipRow(headerFields)
    );
    // ... But now we have another problem ...
}
```

JOIN

Using `.map()` to run `splitFields()` is fine, as `.splitFields()` doesn't return an Either. But when we get to running `zipRow()` we have a problem. Calling `zipRow()` returns an Either. So, if we use `.map()` we end up sticking an Either inside an Either. If we go any further we'll be stuck, unless we run `.map()` inside `.map()`. This isn't going to work so well. We need some way to join those nested Eithers together into one. So, we'll write a new method, called `.join()`:

```
/**
 *Left represents the sad path.
 */
class Left {
    constructor(val) {
        this._val = val;
    }
    map() {
        // Left is the sad path
        // so we do nothing
        return this;
    }
    join() {
        // On the sad path, we don't
        // do anything with join
        return this;
    }
    toString() {
        const str = this._val.toString();
        return `Left(${str})`;
    }
}


/**
 * Right represents the happy path
 */
class Right {
    constructor(val) {
        this._val = val;
    }
```

```
    map(fn) {
        return new Right(
            fn(this._val)
        );
    }
    join() {
        if ((this._val instanceof Left)
            || (this._val instanceof Right))
        {
            return this._val;
        }
        return this;
    }
    toString() {
        const str = this._val.toString();
        return `Right(${str})`;
    }
}
```

Now we're free to un-nest our values:

```
function processRow(headerFields, row) {
    const fieldsEither = right(row).map(splitFields);
    const rowObj = fieldsEither
        .map(zipRow(headerFields))
        .join();
    const rowObjWithDate = rowObj.map(addDateStr).join();
    // Slowly getting better... but what do we return?
}
```

We've made it a lot further. But having to remember to call .join() every time is annoying. This pattern of calling .map() and .join() together is so common that we'll create a shortcut method for it. We'll call it chain() because it allows us to chain together functions that return Left or Right.

```
/**
 *Left represents the sad path.
 */
class Left {
    constructor(val) {
        this._val = val;
    }
    map() {
        // Left is the sad path
        // so we do nothing
        return this;
    }
    join() {
        // On the sad path, we don't
        // do anything with join
        return this;
    }
    chain() {
        // Boring sad path,
        // do nothing.
        return this;
    }
    toString() {
        const str = this._val.toString();
```

```
        return `Left(${str})`;
    }
}
/**
 * Right represents the happy path
 */
class Right {
    constructor(val) {
        this._val = val;
    }
    map(fn) {
        return new Right(
            fn(this._val)
        );
    }
    join() {
        if ((this._val instanceof Left)
            || (this._val instanceof Right)) {
            return this._val;
        }
        return this;
    }
    chain(fn) {
        return fn(this._val);
    }
    toString() {
        const str = this._val.toString();
        return `Right(${str})`;
    }
}
```

Going back to our railway track analogy, .chain() allows us to switch rails if we come across an error. It's easier to show with a diagram though.

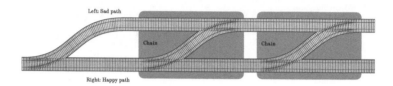

Left: Sad path

Chain

Chain

Right: Happy path

Figure C.3: The .chain() method allows us to switch over to the left track if an error occurs. Note that the switches only go one way.

With that in place, our code is a little clearer:

```
function processRow(headerFields, row) {
    const fieldsEither = right(row).map(splitFields);
    const rowObj = fieldsEither
        .chain(zipRow(headerFields));
    const rowObjWithDate = rowObj.chain(addDateStr);
    // Slowly getting better... but what do we return?
}
```

We're nearly done reworking our processRow() function. But what happens when we return the value? Eventually, we want to take different action depending on whether we have a Left or Right. So we'll write a function that will take different action accordingly:

```
function either(leftFunc, rightFunc, e) {
    return (e instanceof Left)
        ? leftFunc(e._val)
        : rightFunc(e._val);
}
```

We've cheated and used the inner values of the Left or Right objects. But we'll pretend you didn't see that. We're now able to finish our function:

```
function processRow(headerFields, row) {
    const fieldsEither  = right(row).map(splitFields);
    const rowObj  = fieldsEither
        .chain(zipRow(headerFields));
    const rowObjWithDate = rowObj.chain(addDateStr);
    return either(showError, rowToMessage, rowObjWithDate);
}
```

And if we're feeling particularly clever, we could write it using a fluent syntax:

```
function processRow(headerFields, row) {
    const rowObjWithDate = right(row)
        .map(splitFields)
        .chain(zipRow(headerFields))
```

```
        .chain(addDateStr);
    return either(showError, rowToMessage, rowObjWithDate);
}
```

Both versions are pretty neat. Not a try...catch in sight. And
no if-statements in our top-level function. If there's a problem
with any particular row, we just show an error message at the end.
And note that in processRow() the only time we mention Left or
Right is at the very start when we call right(). For the rest, we just
use the .map() and .chain() methods to apply the next function.

AP AND LIFT

This is looking good, but there's one final scenario that we need to
consider. Sticking with the example, let's take a look at how we
might process the whole CSV data, rather than just each row. We'll
need a helper function or three:

```
function splitCSVToRows(csvData) {
    // There should always be a header row... so if there's no
    // newline character, something is wrong.
    return (csvData.indexOf('\n') < 0)
        ? left('No header row found in CSV data')
        : right(csvData.split('\n'));
}


function processRows(headerFields, dataRows) {
    // Note this is Array map, not Either map.
    return dataRows.map(row => processRow(headerFields, row));
}
```

```
function showMessages(messages) {
    return `<ul class="Messages">${messages.join('\n')}</ul>`;
}
```

So, we have a helper function that splits the CSV data into rows.
And we get an Either back. Now, we can use .map() and some lodash
functions to split out the header row from data rows. But we end
up in an interesting situation...

```
function csvToMessages(csvData) {
    const csvRows      = splitCSVToRows(csvData);
    const headerFields = csvRows.map(_.head).map(splitFields);
    const dataRows     = csvRows.map(_.tail);
    // What's next?
}
```

We have our header fields and data rows all ready to map
over with processRows(). But headerFields and dataRows are
both wrapped up inside an Either. We need some way to convert
processRows() to a function that works with Eithers. As a first
step, we will curry processRows.

```
function processRows(headerFields) {
    return function processRowsWithHeaderFields(dataRows) {
        // Note this is Array map, not Either map.
        return dataRows.map(
            row => processRow(headerFields, row)
        );
    };
}
```

Now, with this in place, we can run an experiment. We have

headerFields which is an Either wrapped around an array. What would happen if we were to take headerFields and call `.map()` on it with `processRows()`?

```
function csvToMessages(csvData) {
    const csvRows      = splitCSVToRows(csvData);
    const headerFields = csvRows.map(_.head).map(splitFields);
    const dataRows     = csvRows.map(_.tail);

    // How will we pass headerFields and dataRows to
    // processRows() ?
    const funcInEither = headerFields.map(processRows);
}
```

Using `.map()` here calls the outer function of `processRows()`, but not the inner one. In other words, `processRows()` returns a function. And because it's `.map()`, we still get an Either back. So we end up with a function inside an Either. I gave it away a little with the variable name. `funcInEither` is an Either. It contains a function that takes an array of strings and returns an array of different strings. We need some way to take that function and call it with the value inside `dataRows`. To do that, we need to add one more method to our Left and Right classes. We'll call it `.ap()` because the standard tells us to. The way to remember it is to recall that ap is short for 'apply'. It helps us apply values to functions.

The method for the Left does nothing, as usual:

```
// In Left (the sad path)
ap() {
    return this;
}
```

And for the Right class, the variable name spells out that we expect the other Either to contain a function:

```
// In Right (the happy path)
ap(otherEither) {
    const functionToRun = otherEither._val;
    return this.map(functionToRun);
}
```

So, with that in place, we can finish off our main function:

```
function csvToMessages(csvData) {
    const csvRows      = splitCSVToRows(csvData);
    const headerFields = csvRows.map(_.head).map(splitFields);
    const dataRows     = csvRows.map(_.tail);
    const funcInEither = headerFields.map(processRows);
    const messagesArr  = dataRows.ap(funcInEither);
    return either(showError, showMessages, messagesArr);
}
```

Now, I've mentioned this before, but I find .ap() a little confusing to work with.[2] Another way to think about it is to say: "I have a function that would normally take two plain values. I want to turn it into a function that takes two Eithers". Now that we have .ap(), we can write a function that will do exactly that. We'll call it liftA2(), again because it's a standard name. It takes a plain function expecting two arguments, and 'lifts' it to work with 'Applicatives'. (Applicatives are things that have an .ap() method and an .of() method). So, liftA2 is short for 'lift applicative, two parameters'.

---

[2] This is not helped by the fact that the Fantasyland specification defines .ap() in a confusing way. It uses the reverse order from the way most other languages define it.

So, a `liftA2` function might look something like this:

```
function liftA2(func) {
    return function runApplicativeFunc(a, b) {
        return b.ap(a.map(func));
    };
}
```

So, our top-level function would use it like this:

```
function csvToMessages(csvData) {
    const csvRows      = splitCSVToRows(csvData);
    const headerFields = csvRows.map(_.head).map(splitFields);
    const dataRows     = csvRows.map(_.tail);
    const processRowsA = liftA2(processRows);
    const messagesArr  = processRowsA(headerFields, dataRows);
    return either(showError, showMessages, messagesArr);
}
```

You can see the whole thing in action on CodePen.

§ C.7. REALLY? IS THAT IT?

Now, why is this any better than just throwing exceptions? Does it seem like an overly-complicated way to handle something simple? Well, let's think about why we like exceptions in the first place. If we didn't have exceptions, we would have to write a lot of if-statements all over the place. We would be forever writing code along the lines of 'if the last thing worked keep going, else handle the error'. And we would have to keep handling these errors all through our code. That makes it hard to follow what's going on. Throwing exceptions allows us to jump out of the program flow when something goes wrong. So we don't have to write all those if-statements. We can focus on the happy path.

But there's a catch. Exceptions hide a little too much. When you throw an exception, you make handling the error some other function's problem. It's all too easy to ignore the exception, and let it bubble all the way to the top of the program. The nice thing about Either is that it lets you jump out of the main program flow like you would with an exception. But it's honest about it. You get either a Right or a Left. You can't pretend that Lefts aren't a possibility. Eventually, you have to pull the value out with something like an `either()` call.

Now, I know that sounds like a pain. But take a look at the code we've written (not the Either classes, the functions that use them). There's not a lot of exception handling code there. In fact, there's almost none, except for the `either()` call at the end of `csvToMessages()` and `processRow()`. And that's the point. With Either, you get pure error handling that you can't accidentally forget. But without it stomping through your code and adding indentation everywhere.

This is not to say that you should never ever use `try...catch`. Sometimes that's the right tool for the job, and that's OK. But it's not the *only* tool. Using Either gives us some advantages that `try...catch` can't match. So, perhaps give Either a go sometime. Even if it's tricky at first, I think you'll get to like it. If you do give it a go though, please don't use the implementation from this tutorial. Try one of the well-established libraries like Crocks, Sanctuary, Folktale or Monet. They're better maintained. And I've papered over some things for the sake of simplicity here. If you do give it a go, let me know by sending me a tweet.

- Professor Frisby's Mostly Adequate Guide to Functional Programming by Brian Lonsdorf (and others)
- The Fantasy Land Specification
- Practical Intro to Monads in JavaScript: Either by Jakub Strojewski
- The Marvellously Mysterious JavaScript Maybe Monad by yours truly

HOW TO DEAL WITH DIRTY SIDE EFFECTS IN YOUR PURE FUNCTIONAL JAVASCRIPT

So, you've begun to dabble in functional programming. It won't be long before you come across the concept of *pure functions*. And, as you go on, you will discover that functional programmers appear to be obsessed with them. "Pure functions let you reason about your code," they say. "Pure functions are less likely to start a thermonuclear war." "Pure functions give you referential transparency." And on it goes. They are not wrong either. Pure functions are a good thing. But there's a problem...

A pure function is a function that has no side effects.[1] But if you

---
[1] This is not a complete definition, but will do for the moment. We will come back

know anything about programming, you know that side effects are the *whole point*. Why bother calculating π to 100 places if there's no way anyone can read it? To print it out somewhere, we need to write to a console, or send data to a printer, or *something* where someone can read it. And, what good is a database if you can't enter any data into it? We *need* to read data from input devices, and request information from the network. We can't do any of it without side effects. And yet, functional programming is built around pure functions. So how do functional programmers manage to get anything done?

The short answer is, they do what mathematicians do: They cheat.

Now, when I say they cheat, they technically follow the rules. But they find loopholes in those rules and stretch them big enough to drive a herd of elephants through. There's two main ways they do this:

1. *Dependency injection*, or as I call it, *chucking the problem over the fence*; and
2. *Using an Effect functor*, which I think of as *extreme procrastination*.[2]

§ D.1. DEPENDENCY INJECTION

Dependency injection is our first method for dealing with side effects. In this approach, we take any impurities in our code, and shove them into function parameters. Then we can treat them as some other function's responsibility. To explain what I mean, let's look at some code:[3]

---

to the formal definition later.

[2] In other languages (like Haskell) this is called an IO functor or an IO monad. PureScript uses the term *Effect*. And I find it is a little more descriptive.

[3] A note for those familiar with type signatures. If we were being strict we would need to account for the side-effect here. But we'll get to that a little bit later.

```
// logSomething :: String -> String
function logSomething(something) {
    const dt = (new Date()).toISOString();
    console.log('${dt}: ${something}');
    return something;
}
```

Our `logSomething()` function has two sources of impurity: It
creates a `Date()` and it logs to the console. So, not only does it
perform IO, it also gives a different result every millisecond that
you run it. So, how do you make this function pure? With dependency injection, we take any impurities and make them a function
parameter. So instead of taking one parameter, our function will
take three:

```
// logSomething: Date -> Console -> String -> *
function logSomething(d, cnsl, something) {
    const dt = d.toIsoString();
    return cnsl.log('${dt}: ${something}');
}
```

Then to call it, we have to explicitly pass in the impure bits
ourselves:

```
const something = "Curiouser and curiouser!"
const d = new Date();
logSomething(d, console, something);
// } Curiouser and curiouser!
```

Now, you may be thinking: "This is stupid. All we've done is
shoved the problem one level up. It's still just as impure as before."
And you'd be right. It's totally a loophole.

It's like feigning ignorance: "Oh no officer, I had no idea that calling log() on that "cnsl" object would perform IO. Someone else just passed it to me. I've got no idea where it came from." It seems a bit lame.

It's not quite as stupid as it seems though. Notice something about our logSomething() function. If you want it to do something impure, you have to *make* it impure. We could just as easily pass different parameters:

```
const d = {toISOString: () => '1865-11-26T16:00:00.000Z'};
const cnsl = {
    log: () => {
        // do nothing
    },
};
logSomething(d, cnsl, "Off with their heads!");
// ← "Off with their heads!"
```

Now, our function does nothing (other than return the something parameter). But it is completely pure. If you call it with those same parameters, it will return the same thing every single time. And that is the point. To make it impure, we have to take deliberate action. Or, to put it another way, everything that function depends on is right there in the signature. It doesn't access any global objects like console or Date. It makes everything explicit.

It's also important to note, that we can pass functions to our formerly impure function too. Let's look at another example. Imagine we have a username in a form somewhere. We'd like to get the value of that form input:

```
// getUserNameFromDOM :: () -> String
function getUserNameFromDOM() {
    return document.querySelector('#username').value;
}


const username = getUserNameFromDOM();
username;
// ← "mhatter"
```

In this case, we're attempting to query the DOM for some information. This is impure, since document is a global object that could change at any moment. One way to make our function pure would be to pass the global document object as a parameter. But, we could also pass a querySelector() function like so:

```
// getUserNameFromDOM :: (String -> Element) -> String
function getUserNameFromDOM($) {
    return $('#username').value;
}


// qs :: String -> Element
const qs = document.querySelector.bind(document);

const username = getUserNameFromDOM(qs);
username;
// ← "mhatter"
```

Now, again, you may be thinking "This is still stupid!" All we've done is move the impurity out of getUsernameFromDOM(). It hasn't gone away. We've just stuck it in another function qs(). It doesn't seem to do much other than make the code longer. Instead of one impure function, we have two functions, one of which is still impure.

Bear with me. Imagine we want to write a test for `getUserNameFromDOM()`. Now, comparing the impure and pure versions, which one would be easier to work with? For the impure version to work at all, we need a global document object. And on top of that, it needs to have an element with the ID `username` somewhere inside it. If I want to test that outside a browser, then I have to import something like JSDOM or a headless browser. All to test one very small function. But using the second version, I can do this:

```
const qsStub = () => ({value: 'mhatter'});
const username = getUserNameFromDOM(qsStub);
assert.strictEqual(
    'mhatter',
    username,
    `Expected username to be ${username}`
);
```

Now, this doesn't mean that you shouldn't also create an integration test that runs in a real browser. (Or, at least a simulated one like JSDOM). But what this example does show is that `getUserNameFromDOM()` is now completely predictable. If we pass it qsStub it will always return `mhatter`. We've moved the unpredictability into the smaller function qs.

If we want to, we can keep pushing that unpredictability further and further out. Eventually, we push them right to the very edges of our code. So we end up with a thin shell of impure code that wraps around a well-tested, predictable core. As you start to build larger applications, that predictability starts to matter. A lot.

It is possible to create large, complex applications this way. I know because I've done it. Testing becomes easier, and it makes every function's dependencies explicit. But it does have some drawbacks. The main one is that you end up with lengthy function signatures like this:

```
function app(doc, con, ftch, store, config, ga, d, random) {
    // Application code goes here
}


app(
    document,
    console,
    fetch,
    store,
    config,
    ga,
    (new Date()),
    Math.random
);
```

This isn't so bad, except that you then have the issue of parameter drilling. You might need one those parameters in a very low-level function. So you have to thread the parameter down through many layers of function calls. It gets annoying. For example, you might have to pass the date down through 5 layers of intermediate functions. And none of those intermediate functions uses the date object at all. It's not the end of the world. And it is good to be able to see those explicit dependencies. But it's still annoying. And there is another way...

Let's look at the second loophole that functional programmers exploit. It starts like this: *A side effect isn't a side effect until it actually happens.* Sounds cryptic, I know. Let's try and make that a bit clearer. Consider this code:

```
// fZero :: () -> Number
function fZero() {
    console.log('Launching nuclear missiles');
    // Code to launch nuclear missiles goes here
    return 0;
}
```

It's a stupid example, I know. If we want a zero in our code, we can just write it. And I know you, gentle reader, would never write code to control nuclear weapons in JavaScript. But it helps illustrate the point. This is clearly impure code. It logs to the console, and it might also start thermonuclear war. Imagine we want that zero though. Imagine a scenario where we want to calculate something *after* missile launch. We might need to start a countdown timer or something like that. In this scenario, it would be perfectly reasonable to plan out how we'd do that calculation ahead of time. And we would want to be very careful about when those missiles take off. We don't want to mix up our calculations in such a way that they might accidentally launch the missiles. So, what if we wrapped fZero() inside another function that just returned it. Kind of like a safety wrapper.

```
// fZero :: () -> Number
function fZero() {
    console.log('Launching nuclear missiles');
```

```
    // Code to launch nuclear missiles goes here
    return 0;
}


// returnZeroFunc :: () -> (() -> Number)
function returnZeroFunc() {
    return fZero;
}
```

I can run `returnZeroFunc()` as many times as I want, and so long as I don't *call* the return value, I am (theoretically) safe. My code won't launch any nuclear missiles.

```
const zeroFunc1 = returnZeroFunc();
const zeroFunc2 = returnZeroFunc();
const zeroFunc3 = returnZeroFunc();
// No nuclear missiles launched.
```

Now, let's define pure functions a bit more formally. Then we can examine our `returnZeroFunc()` function in more detail. A function is pure if:

1. It has no observable side effects; and
2. It is referentially transparent. That is, given the same input it always returns the same output.

Let's check out `returnZeroFunc()`. Does it have any side effects? Well, we just established that calling `returnZeroFunc()` won't launch any nuclear missiles. Unless you go to the extra step of calling the returned function, nothing happens. So, no side-effects here.

Is it `returnZeroFunc()` referentially transparent? That is, does it always return the same value given the same input? Well, the way it's currently written, we can test it:

```
zeroFunc1 === zeroFunc2; // true
zeroFunc2 === zeroFunc3; // true
```

But it's not quite pure yet. Our function `returnZeroFunc()` is referencing a variable outside its scope. To solve that, we can rewrite it this way:

```
// returnZeroFunc :: () -> (() -> Number)
function returnZeroFunc() {
    function fZero() {
        console.log('Launching nuclear missiles');
        // Code to launch nuclear missiles goes here
        return 0;
    }
    return fZero;
}
```

Our function is now pure. But, JavaScript works against us a little here. We can't use `===` to verify referential transparency any more. This is because `returnZeroFunc()` will return always a new function reference. But you can check referential transparency by inspecting the code. Our `returnZeroFunc()` function does nothing other than return the *same* function, every time.

This is a neat little loophole. But can we actually use it for real code? The answer is yes. But before we get to how you'd do it in practice, let's push this idea a little further. Going back to our dangerous `fZero()` function:

```
// fZero :: () -> Number
function fZero() {
    console.log('Launching nuclear missiles');
    // Code to launch nuclear missiles goes here
    return 0;
}
```

Let's try and use the zero that fZero() returns, but without starting thermonuclear war (yet). We'll create a function that takes the zero that fZero() eventually returns, and adds one to it:

```
// fIncrement :: (() -> Number) -> Number
function fIncrement(f) {
    return f() + 1;
}


fIncrement(fZero);
// ) Launching nuclear missiles
// ← 1
```

Whoops. We accidentally started thermonuclear war. Let's try again. This time, we won't return a number. Instead, we'll return a function that will *eventually* return a number:

```
// fIncrement :: (() -> Number) -> (() -> Number)
function fIncrement(f) {
    return () => f() + 1;
}


fIncrement(zero);
// ← [Function]
```

Phew. Crisis averted. Let's keep going. With these two functions, we can create a whole bunch of 'eventual numbers':

```javascript
const fOne   = fIncrement(zero);
const fTwo   = fIncrement(one);
const fThree = fIncrement(two);
// And so on...
```

We could also create a bunch of f*() functions that work with eventual values:

```javascript
// fMultiply ::
// (() -> Number)
// -> (() -> Number)
// -> (() -> Number)
function fMultiply(a, b) {
    return () => a() * b();
}


// fPow :: (() -> Number) -> (() -> Number) -> (() -> Number)
function fPow(a, b) {
    return () => Math.pow(a(), b());
}


// fSqrt :: (() -> Number) -> (() -> Number)
function fSqrt(x) {
    return () => Math.sqrt(x());
}


const fFour = fPow(fTwo, fTwo);
const fEight = fMultiply(fFour, fTwo);
```

```
const fTwentySeven = fPow(fThree, fThree);
const fNine = fSqrt(fTwentySeven);
// No console log or thermonuclear war. Jolly good show!
```

Do you see what we've done here? Anything we would do with regular numbers, we can do with eventual numbers. Mathematicians call this 'isomorphism'. We can always turn a regular number into an eventual number by sticking it in a function. And we can get the eventual number back by calling the function. In other words we have a *mapping* between numbers and eventual numbers. It's more exciting than it sounds. I promise. We'll come back to this idea soon.

This function wrapping thing is a legitimate strategy. We can keep hiding behind functions as long as we want. And so long as we never actually call any of these functions, they're all theoretically pure. And nobody is starting any wars. In regular (non-nuclear) code, we actually *want* those side effects, eventually. Wrapping everything in a function lets us control those effects with precision. We decide exactly when those side effects happen. But, it's a pain typing those brackets everywhere. And it's annoying to create new versions of every function. We've got perfectly good functions like Math.sqrt() built into the language. It would be nice if there was a way to use those ordinary functions with our delayed values. Enter the Effect functor.

§ D.3. THE EFFECT FUNCTOR

For our purposes, the Effect functor is nothing more than an object that we stick our delayed function in. So, we'll stick our fZero function into an Effect object. But, before we do that, let's take the pressure down a notch:

```javascript
// zero :: () -> Number
function fZero() {
    console.log('Starting with nothing');
    // Definitely not launching a nuclear strike here.
    // But this function is still impure.
    return 0;
}
```

Now we create a constructor function that creates an Effect object for us:

```javascript
// Effect :: Function -> Effect
function Effect(f) {
    return {};
}
```

Not much to look at so far. Let's make it do something useful. We want to use our regular `fZero()` function with our Effect. We'll write a method that will take a regular function, and *eventually* apply it to our delayed value. And we'll do it *without triggering the effect*. We call it map. This is because it creates a *mapping* between regular functions and Effect functions. It might look something like this:

```javascript
// Effect :: Function -> Effect
function Effect(f) {
    return {
        map(g) {
            return Effect(x => g(f(x)));
        }
    }
```

```
        }
```

Now, if you're paying attention, you may be wondering about map(). It looks suspiciously like compose. We'll come back to that later. For now, let's try it out:

```
const zero = Effect(fZero);
const increment = x => x + 1; // A plain ol' regular function.
const one = zero.map(increment);
```

Hmm. We don't really have a way to see what happened. Let's modify Effect so we have a way to 'pull the trigger', so to speak:

```
// Effect :: Function -> Effect
function Effect(f) {
    return {
        map(g) {
            return Effect(x => g(f(x)));
        },
        runEffects(x) {
            return f(x);
        }
    }
}

const zero = Effect(fZero);
const increment = x => x + 1; // Just a regular function.
const one = zero.map(increment);

one.runEffects();
// ] Starting with nothing
```

And if we want to, we can keep calling that map function:

```
const double = x => x * 2;
const cube = x => Math.pow(x, 3);
const eight = Effect(fZero)
    .map(increment)
    .map(double)
    .map(cube);

eight.runEffects();
// ) Starting with nothing
// ← 8
```

Now, this is where it starts to get interesting. We called this a 'functor'. All that means is that Effect has a map function, and it obeys some rules. These rules aren't the kind of rules for things you *can't* do though. They're rules for things you *can* do. They're more like privileges. Because Effect is part of the functor club, there are certain things it gets to do. One of those is called the 'composition rule'. It goes like this:

> If we have an Effect e, and two functions f, and g
> Then e.map(g).map(f) is equivalent to e.map(x => f(g(x))).

To put it another way, doing two maps in a row is equivalent to composing the two functions. Which means Effect can do things like this (recall our example above):

```
const incDoubleCube = x => cube(double(increment(x)));
// If we're using a library like Ramda or lodash/fp we could
// also write:
```

```
// const incDoubleCube = compose(cube, double, increment);
const eight = Effect(fZero).map(incDoubleCube);
```

And when we do that, we are *guaranteed* to get the same result as our triple-map version. We can use this to refactor our code, with confidence that our code will not break. In some cases we can even make performance improvements by swapping between approaches.

But enough with the number examples. Let's do something more like 'real' code.

A SHORTCUT FOR MAKING EFFECTS

Our Effect constructor takes a function as its argument. This is convenient, because most of the side effects we want to delay are also functions. For example, Math.random() and console.log() are both this type of thing. But sometimes we want to jam a plain old value into an Effect. For example, imagine we've attached some sort of config object to the window global in the browser. We want to get a value out, but this is will not be a pure operation. We can write a little shortcut that will make this task easier:[4]

```
// of :: a -> Effect a
Effect.of = function of(val) {
    return Effect(() => val);
}
```

To show how this might be handy, imagine we're working on a web application. This application has some standard features like a list of articles and a user bio. But *where* in the HTML these com-

---

[4] Note that different languages have different names for this shortcut. In Haskell, for example, it's called pure. I have no idea why.

ponents live changes for different customers. Since we're clever engineers, we decide to store their locations in a global config object. That way we can always locate them. For example:

```
window.myAppConf = {
    selectors: {
        'user-bio':     '.userbio',
        'article-list': '#articles',
        'user-name':    '.userfullname',
    },
    templates: {
        'greet':  'Pleased to meet you, {name}',
        'notify': 'You have {n} alerts',
    }
};
```

Now, with our `Effect.of()` shortcut, we can quickly shove the value we want into an Effect wrapper like so:

```
const win = Effect.of(window);
userBioLocator = win.map(
    x => x.myAppConf.selectors['user-bio']
);
// ← Effect('.userbio')
```

NESTING AND UN-NESTING EFFECTS

Mapping Effects thing can get us a long way. But sometimes we end up mapping a function that also returns an Effect. We've already defined `getElementLocator()` which returns an Effect containing a string. If we actually want to locate the DOM element, then we need to call `document.querySelector()`—another impure function.

So we might purify it by returning an Effect instead:

```
// $ :: String -> Effect DOMElement
function $(selector) {
    return Effect.of(document.querySelector(s));
}
```

Now if we want to put those two together, we can try using map():

```
const userBio = userBioLocator.map($);
// ← Effect(Effect(<div>))
```

What we've got is a bit awkward to work with now. If we want to access that div, we have to map with a function that also maps the thing we actually want to do. For example, if we wanted to get the innerHTML it would look something like this:

```
const innerHTML = userBio.map(
    eff => eff.map(domEl => domEl.innerHTML)
);
// ← Effect(Effect('<h2>User Biography</h2>'))
```

Let's try picking that apart a little. We'll back all the way up to userBio and move forward from there. It will be a bit tedious, but we want to be clear about what's going on here. The notation we've been using, Effect('user-bio') is a little misleading. If we were to write it as code, it would look more like so:

```
Effect(() => '.userbio');
```

Except that's not accurate either. What we're really doing is more like:

```
Effect(() => window.myAppConf.selectors['user-bio']);
```

Now, when we map, it's the same as composing that inner function with another function (as we saw above). So when we map with $, it looks a bit like so:

```
Effect(() => $(window.myAppConf.selectors['user-bio']));
```

Expanding that out gives us:

```
Effect(
    () => Effect.of(
        document.querySelector(
            window.myAppConf.selectors['user-bio']
        )
    )
);
```

And expanding Effect.of gives us a clearer picture:

```
Effect(
    () => Effect(
        () => document.querySelector(
            window.myAppConf.selectors['user-bio']
        )
    )
);
```

Note: All the code that actually does stuff is in the innermost function. None of it has leaked out to the outer Effect.

Join

Why bother spelling all that out? Well, we want to un-nest these nested Effects. If we're going to do that, we want to make certain that we're not bringing in any unwanted side-effects in the process. For Effect, the way to un-nest, is to call .runEffects() on the outer function. But this might get confusing. We've gone through this whole exercise to check that we're *not* going to run any effects. So we'll create another function that does the same thing, and call it join. We use join when we're un-nesting Effects, and runEffects() when we actually want to run effects. That makes our intention clear, even if the code we run is the same.

```
// Effect :: Function -> Effect
function Effect(f) {
    return {
        map(g) {
            return Effect(x => g(f(x)));
        },
        runEffects(x) {
            return f(x);
        }
        join(x) {
            return f(x);
        }
    }
}
```

We can then use this to un-nest our user biography element:

```
const userBioHTML = Effect.of(window)
    .map(x => x.myAppConf.selectors['user-bio'])
    .map($)
    .join()
    .map(x => x.innerHTML);
// ← Effect('<h2>User Biography</h2>')
```

Chain

This pattern of running .map() followed by .join() comes up often.
So often in fact, that it would be handy to have a shortcut function.
That way, whenever we have a function that returns an Effect, we
can use this shortcut. It saves us writing map then join over and
over. We'd write it like so:

```
// Effect :: Function -> Effect
function Effect(f) {
    return {
        map(g) {
            return Effect(x => g(f(x)));
        },
        runEffects(x) {
            return f(x);
        }
        join(x) {
            return f(x);
        }
        chain(g) {
            return Effect(f).map(g).join();
        }
    }
```

}

We call the new function chain() because it allows us to chain together Effects. (That, and because the standard tells us to call it that).[5] Our code to get the user biography inner HTML would then look more like this:

```
const userBioHTML = Effect.of(window)
    .map(x => x.myAppConf.selectors['user-bio'])
    .chain($)
    .map(x => x.innerHTML);
// ← Effect('<h2>User Biography</h2>')
```

Unfortunately, other programming languages use a bunch of different names for this idea. It can get a little bit confusing if you're trying to read up about it. Sometimes it's called flatMap. This name makes a lot of sense, as we're doing a regular mapping, then flattening out the result with .join(). In Haskell though, it's given the confusing name of bind. So if you're reading elsewhere, keep in mind that chain, flatMap and bind refer to similar concepts.

COMBINING EFFECTS

There's one final scenario where working with Effect might get a little awkward. It's where we want to combine two or more Effects using a single function. For example, what if we wanted to grab the user's name from the DOM? And then insert it into a template provided by our app config? So, we might have a template function like this (note that we're creating a curried[6] version):

---

[5] In this case, the standard is the Fantasy Land specification for Chain.
[6] If you've not come across currying before, check out part 4 of 'A Gentle Introduction to Functional Programming in JavaScript'

```
// tpl :: String -> Object -> String
const tpl = curry(function tpl(pattern, data) {
    return Object.keys(data).reduce(
        (str, key) => str.replace(
            new RegExp(`\{${key}\}`, data[key]),
            pattern
        )
    )
});
```

That's all well and good. But let's grab our data:

```
const win = Effect.of(window);
const name = win
    .map(w => w.myAppConfig.selectors['user-name'])
    .chain($)
    .map(el => el.innerHTML)
    .map(str => ({name: str}));
// ← Effect({name: 'Mr. Hatter'});

const pattern = win
    .map(w => w.myAppConfig.templates('greeting'));
// ← Effect('Pleased to meet you, {name}');
```

We've got a template function. It takes a string and an object, and returns a string. But our string and object (name and pattern) are wrapped up in Effects. What we want to do is *lift* our tpl() function up into a higher plane so that it works with Effects.

Let's start out by seeing what happens if we call map() with tpl() on our pattern Effect:

```
pattern.map(tpl);
// ← Effect([Function])
```

Looking at the types might make things a little clearer. The type signature for map is something like this:

map :: Effect a ~> (a → b) → Effect b

And our template function has the signature:

tpl :: String → Object → String

So, when we call map on `pattern`, we get a *partially applied* function (remember we curried `tpl`) inside an Effect.

Effect (Object → String)

We now want to pass in the value from inside our pattern Effect. But we don't really have a way to do that yet. We'll write another method for Effect (called `ap()`) that will take care of this:

```
// Effect :: Function -> Effect
function Effect(f) {
    return {
        map(g) {
            return Effect(x => g(f(x)));
        },
        runEffects(x) {
            return f(x);
        }
        join(x) {
            return f(x);
        }
        chain(g) {
            return Effect(f).map(g).join();
        }
        ap(eff) {
```

```
                    // If someone calls ap, we assume eff has a
                    // function inside it (rather than a value).
                    // We'll use map to go inside off, and access
                    // that function (we'll call it 'g') Once we've
                    // got g, we apply the value inside off f() to it
            return eff.map(g => g(f()));
        }
    }
}
```

With that in place, we can run `.ap()` to apply our template:

```
const win = Effect.of(window);
const name = win
    .map(w => w.myAppConfig.selectors['user-name'])
    .chain($)
    .map(el => el.innerHTML)
    .map(str => ({name: str}));

const pattern = win
    .map(w => w.myAppConfig.templates('greeting'));

const greeting = name.ap(pattern.map(tpl));
// ⤶ Effect('Pleased to meet you, Mr Hatter')
```

We've achieved our goal. But I have a confession to make... The thing is, I find ap() confusing sometimes. It's hard to remember that I have to map the function in first, and then run ap() after. And then I forget which order the parameters are applied. But there is a way around this. Most of the time, what I'm trying to do is *lift* an ordinary function up into the world of applicatives. That is, I've got plain functions, and I want to make them work with things like Effect that have an `.ap()` method. We can write a function that will do this for us:

```
// liftA2 :: (a -> b -> c) ->
//     (Applicative a -> Applicative b -> Applicative c)
const liftA2 = curry(function liftA2(f, x, y) {
    return y.ap(x.map(f));
    // We could also write:
    //   return x.map(f).chain(g => y.map(g));
});
```

We've called it `liftA2()` because it lifts a function that takes two arguments. We could similarly write a `liftA5()` like so:

```
// liftA5 :: (a -> b -> c -> d) ->
// (Applicative a ->
//   Applicative b ->
//   Applicative c ->
//   Applicative d)
const liftA5 = curry(function liftA5(f, a, b, c) {
    return c.ap(b.ap(a.map(f)));
});
```

Notice that `liftA2` and `liftA5` don't ever mention Effect. In theory, they can work with any object that has a compatible `ap()` method.

Using `liftA2()` we can rewrite our example above as follows:

```
const win = Effect.of(window);
const user = win
    .map(w => w.myAppConfig.selectors['user-name'])
    .chain($)
```

```
    .map(el => el.innerHTML)
    .map(str => ({name: str}));

const pattern = win
    .map(w => w.myAppConfig.templates['greeting']);

const greeting = liftA2(tpl)(pattern, user);
// ← Effect('Pleased to meet you, Mr Hatter')
```

§ D.4. SO WHAT?

At this point, you may be thinking 'This seems like a lot of effort to go to just to avoid the odd side effect here and there.' What does it matter? Sticking things inside Effects, and wrapping our heads around `ap()` seems like hard work. Why bother, when the impure code works just fine? And when would you ever *need* this in the real world?

> The functional programmer sounds rather like a mediæval monk, denying himself the pleasures of life in the hope it will make him virtuous.

—John Hughes[7]

Let's break those objections down into two questions:

1. Does functional purity really matter? and
2. When would this Effect thing ever be useful in the real world?

---

[7] John Hughes, 1990, 'Why Functional Programming Matters', *Research Topics in Functional Programming* ed. D. Turner, Addison-Wesley, pp 17–42, https://www.cs.kent.ac.uk/people/staff/dat/miranda/whyfp90.pdf

It's true. When you look at a small function in isolation, a little bit of impurity doesn't matter. Writing `const pattern = window.myAppConfig.templates['greeting'];` is quicker and simpler than something like this:

```
const pattern = Effect
    .of(window)
    .map(w => w.myAppConfig.templates('greeting'));
```

And *if that was all you ever did*, that would remain true. The side effect wouldn't matter. But this is just one line of code—in an application that may contain thousands, even millions of lines of code. Functional purity starts to matter a lot more when you're trying to work out why your app has mysteriously stopped working 'for no reason'. Something unexpected has happened. You're trying to break the problem down and isolate its cause. In those circumstances, the more code you can rule out the better. If your functions are pure, then you can be confident that the only thing affecting their behaviour are the inputs passed to it. And this narrows down the number of things you need to consider... err... considerably. In other words, it allows you to *think less*. In a large, complex application, this is a Big Deal.

THE EFFECT PATTERN IN THE REAL WORLD

Okay. Maybe functional purity matters if you're building a large, complex applications. Something like Facebook or Gmail. But what if you're not doing that? Let's consider a scenario that will become more and more common. You have some data. Not just a little bit of data, but a *lot* of data. Millions of rows of it, in CSV text files, or huge database tables. And you're tasked with processing this data. Perhaps you're training an artificial neural network to build an inference model. Perhaps you're trying to figure out the next big cryptocurrency move. Whatever. The thing is, it's going to take a lot of processing grunt to get the job done.

Joel Spolsky argues convincingly that functional programming can help us out here. We could write alternative versions of `map` and `reduce` that will run in parallel. And functional purity makes this possible. But that's not the end of the story. Sure, you can write some fancy parallel processing code. But even then, your development machine still only has 4 cores (or maybe 8 or 16 if you're lucky). That job is still going to take forever. Unless, that is, you can run it on *heaps* of processors... something like a GPU, or a whole cluster of processing servers.

For this to work, you'd need to *describe* the computations you want to run. But, you want to describe them *without actually running them.* Sound familiar? Ideally, you'd then pass the description to some sort of framework. The framework would take care of reading all the data in, and splitting it up among processing nodes. Then the same framework would pull the results back together and tell you how it went. This how TensorFlow works.

> TensorFlow™ is an open source software library for high performance numerical computation. Its flexible architecture allows easy deployment of computation across a variety of platforms (CPUs, GPUs, TPUs), and from desktops to clusters of servers to mobile and edge devices. Originally developed by researchers and engineers from the Google Brain team within Google's AI organization, it comes with strong support for machine learning and deep learning and the flexible numerical computation core is used across many other scientific domains.
>
> —TensorFlow home page[8]

---

[8] *TensorFlow™: An open source machine learning framework for everyone,* https:

When you use TensorFlow, you don't use the normal data types from the programming language you're writing in. Instead, you create 'Tensors'. If we wanted to add two numbers, it would look something like this:

```
node1 = tf.constant(3.0, tf.float32)
node2 = tf.constant(4.0, tf.float32)
node3 = tf.add(node1, node2)
```

The above code is written in Python, but it doesn't look so very different from JavaScript, does it? And like with our Effect, the add code won't run until we tell it to (using sess.run(), in this case):

```
print("node3: ", node3)
print("sess.run(node3): ", sess.run(node3))
## ] node3:  Tensor("Add_2:0", shape=(), dtype=float32)
## ] sess.run(node3):  7.0
```

We don't get 7.0 until we call sess.run(). As you can see, it's much the same as our delayed functions. We plan out our computations ahead of time. Then, once we're ready, we pull the trigger to kick everything off.

§ D.5. SUMMARY

We've covered a lot of ground. But we've explored two ways to handle functional impurity in our code:

1. Dependency injection; and
2. The Effect functor.

Dependency injection works by moving the impure parts of the

//www.tensorflow.org/, 12 May 2018.

code out of the function. So you have to pass them in as parameters. The Effect functor, in contrast, works by wrapping everything behind a function. To run the effects, we have to make a deliberate effort to run the wrapper function.

Both approaches are cheats. They don't remove the impurities entirely, they just shove them out to the edges of our code. But this is a good thing. It makes explicit which parts of the code are impure. This can be a real advantage when attempting to debug problems in complex code bases.

RECURSION
PERFORMANCE
MEASUREMENTS

Listed below are the numbers used to generate the charts in Chapter 4. I've included them here in the interest of transparency and accessibility. But, in truth, they're not terribly interesting on their own. They make most sense when considered in context, as discussed in the chapter.

§ E.1. RECURSIVE ARRAY MAP PERFORMANCE

These tables document the amount of time taken to process an array of varying length using three different recursive algorithms.

Table E.1: Recursive Array Map performance (microseconds per operation). MacBook Pro (16-inch, 2019), 2.6 GHz 6-Core Intel Core i7. **Chrome 104.0.**

Array Elements	Plain Recursive	Tail Call	Trampoline
100	52.35	35.56	40.23
200	234.33	135.36	153.50
300	621.71	347.20	355.37
400	1154.08	601.69	799.73
500	2007.51	904.02	1239.86
600	4019.45	1318.06	2162.63
700	6250.78	1763.33	2984.63
800	8402.66	2259.78	3764.64
900	10940.92	2917.24	5698.01
1000	13676.15	3576.28	6907.51

Table E.2: Recursive Array Map performance (microseconds per operation). MacBook Pro (16-inch, 2019), 2.6 GHz 6-Core Intel Core i7. **Firefox 104.0**

Array Elements	Plain Recursive	Tail Call	Trampoline
100	134.03	137.50	128.86
200	561.54	524.28	503.19
300	1448.81	1273.22	1218.19
400	2775.31	2613.15	2328.83
500	3696.72	5047.45	3460.93
600	5319.43	7146.94	6158.39
700	7621.37	9914.73	10631.51
800	9703.09	12677.48	14251.10
900	11991.85	10760.79	11064.39
1000	14405.07	13044.61	13693.00

Table E.3: Recursive Array Map performance (microseconds per operation). MacBook Pro (16-inch, 2019), 2.6 GHz 6-Core Intel Core i7. **Safari 15.6.1**

Array Elements	Plain Recursive	Tail Call	Trampoline
100	86.38	86.09	96.45
200	426.74	535.70	400.06
300	1147.28	1194.64	1188.54
400	2102.56	2123.91	2126.35
500	3255.10	3202.25	3451.13
600	4808.85	4615.74	5096.06
700	6500.26	6402.46	7275.90
800	9310.12	8223.01	10487.68
900	12471.94	10870.75	13041.21
1000	15625.00	13095.86	16564.52

§ E.2. RECURSIVE ARRAY MAP PERFORMANCE WITH IMMUTABLE DATA STRUCTURES

Like the last section, these tables document the amount of time taken to process an array of varying length using three different recursive algorithms. But this time, they use an immutable data structure from Immutable JS.

Table E.4: Recursive Array Map performance with Immutable Data Structures (microseconds per operation). MacBook Pro (16-inch, 2019), 2.6 GHz 6-Core Intel Core i7. **Chrome 104.0.**

Array Elements	Plain Recursive	Tail Call	Trampoline
100	5.13	22.84	23.63
200	10.20	45.92	48.02
300	15.55	70.67	71.32

Array Elements	Plain Recursive	Tail Call	Trampoline
400	19.95	91.09	88.33
500	26.30	119.63	120.29
600	30.70	133.98	132.53
700	35.03	162.23	150.70
800	44.21	194.96	198.20
900	44.56	204.85	206.55
1000	52.56	252.01	231.01

Table E.5: Recursive Array Map performance with Immutable Data Structures (microseconds per operation). MacBook Pro (16-inch, 2019), 2.6 GHz 6-Core Intel Core i7 **Firefox 104.0.**

Array Elements	Plain Recursive	Tail Call	Trampoline
100	19.46	53.77	72.17
200	39.15	106.30	116.93
300	59.20	160.89	200.99
400	85.46	223.29	241.52
500	105.93	272.66	319.88
600	122.10	327.08	348.11
700	137.67	372.94	407.46
800	155.82	462.72	516.23
900	185.72	497.95	546.13
1000	206.81	552.50	608.39

Table E.6: Recursive Array Map performance with Immutable Data Structures (microseconds per operation). MacBook Pro (16-inch, 2019), 2.6 GHz 6-Core Intel Core i7. **Safari 15.6.1.**

Array Elements	Plain Recursive	Tail Call	Trampoline
100	9.31	36.69	39.69
200	20.26	78.56	80.00
300	31.63	120.43	115.69
400	43.29	161.77	157.17
500	54.99	199.12	198.71
600	66.16	245.49	230.38
700	78.05	281.44	271.87
800	88.92	320.24	305.01
900	99.25	381.26	349.65
1000	106.76	424.33	402.33

§ E.3.   RECURSIVE DOM TRAVERSAL

These tables describe the time taken to traverse a DOM tree. Each row in the table represents a different depth of tree. Each table represents results for a different browser.

Table E.7: Recursive DOM traversal (microseconds per operation, lower is better). MacBook Pro (16-inch, 2019), 2.6 GHz 6-Core Intel Core i7. **Chrome 104.0.**

Depth	Plain Recursive	Tail Call	Trampoline
100	788.71	216.76	213.24
200	2659.86	447.71	451.54
300	5525.47	719.68	740.97
400	9547.45	982.84	1015.15
500	15248.55	1439.86	1312.03

Depth	Plain Recursive	Tail Call	Trampoline
600	21376.66	2076.37	1772.80
700	25920.17	3095.02	2736.13
800	33322.23	5503.58	3804.89
900	39123.63	9273.00	5296.33
1000	44662.80	14273.48	6990.56
1100	49950.05	17908.31	8692.63
1200	55126.79	22114.11	10610.08
1300	60753.34	28384.90	12570.71
1400	69300.07	34602.08	14351.32
1500	71174.38	41254.13	17185.08

Table E.8: Recursive DOM traversal (microseconds per operation, lower is better). MacBook Pro (16-inch, 2019), 2.6 GHz 6-Core Intel Core i7. **Firefox 104.0**.

Depth	Plain Recursive	Tail Call	Trampoline
100	243.45	204.40	216.39
200	803.81	540.57	552.21
300	1656.92	1040.29	1094.20
400	2885.92	1728.25	1758.98
500	4029.01	2513.07	2473.29
600	5545.39	3866.23	3851.34
700	7163.32	7367.03	7707.72
800	8387.85	11630.61	12733.99
900	9798.16	18681.11	19630.94
1000	10802.64	31046.26	28401.02
1100	12724.27	43233.90	37693.18
1200	15243.90	64724.92	51413.88
1300	15576.32	118203.31	61728.40

Depth	Plain Recursive	Tail Call	Trampoline
1400	20333.47	123762.38	79176.56
1500	18993.35	144300.14	94161.96

Table E.9: Recursive DOM traversal (microseconds per operation, lower is better). MacBook Pro (16-inch, 2019), 2.6 GHz 6-Core Intel Core i7. **Safari 15.6.1.**

Depth	Plain Recursive	Tail Call	Trampoline
100	143.94	166.22	182.94
200	396.71	376.94	371.26
300	712.85	668.16	715.01
400	1203.14	1119.97	1246.32
500	2279.57	1764.01	1789.10
600	2928.69	3916.35	3767.47
700	4136.68	8039.23	11595.55
800	5738.88	17494.75	23282.89
900	10045.20	26075.62	22321.43
1000	9977.05	48192.77	41339.40
1100	24912.81	55126.79	47984.64
1200	29129.04	69589.42	110987.79
1300	19952.11	100300.90	95057.03
1400	32372.94	139470.01	177619.89
1500	17642.91	152671.76	120048.02

ACKNOWLEDGEMENTS

I owe a debt of gratitude to lots of people who helped me with this book. First, thank you to Moritz Grauel, Zenghao He, Kyle Simpson, and James Forbes for reviewing early versions of the book. I appreciate the thoughtful feedback, corrections, and advice you all provided.

Also, thanks to Jason Sheehy for being a consistent encouragement, and patiently listening to me drone on about it. Thanks also to the Reylo Rens team at Atlassian for generally encouraging me, and cheering me on.

Thanks to my friend Eddie for always talking me up, and for trying to buy the book even before it was published.

And last of all, thanks to my wonderful, talented wife, Summer, who assisted with the cover design, and supported me pursuing my dream.

**

Soli deo gloria.